More Aster(ix) Anthologies

The Ferrante Project
October 2020

The Poetry Issue
Winter 2020

Inheritance
Summer 2019

(Un)bound
[double issue]
Winter 2018/2019

Edges
Fall 2018

Dirty Laundry
Fall 2017

Kitchen Table Translation
Summer 2017

Best of Kweli
Spring 2017

What We Love
Fall 2016

Atravesando
Spring 2016

available for order wherever books are sold

and don't forget to visit
asterixjournal.com
for more content and information

Aster(ix) Journal

www.asterixjournal.com

Aster(ix) print issues are usually published 2-3 times a year in print with additional content online. **Aster(ix)** is funded in part by the Dietrich School of Arts and Sciences and the Department of English at University of Pittsburgh.

Aster(ix) Journal

presents

Best of *Hot Metal Bridge*

2007-2020

Edited by
Lorraine Avila, Kleaver Cruz, Lisette Escariz,
K. Henderson, Willie Kinard III, Paola Liendo,
Aeriel Merillat, Gabrielle Ralambo-Rajerison,
Tanya Shirazi, and Amanda Tien

Summer 2021

BLUE SKETCH PRESS | PITTSBURGH

See pg. 166 for individual acknowledgments.

Published via Blue Sketch Press, Pittsburgh.
www.bluesketchpress.com

Best of *Hot Metal Bridge*: 2007-2020
An Aster(ix) Anthology / Aster(ix) Journal
Edited by Willie Kinard III, Aeriel Merillat, & Tanya Shirazi (et al.)—1st ed.

ISBN (print) 978-1-942547-14-3 (trade paperback)
1-942547-14-3 (ISBN-10)

Cover art by Willie Kinard III
Cover Design by Little Owl Creative

First Edition: July 2021

Printed in the United States of America
9 8 7 6 5 4 3 2 1

Thank you to all the graduate students at the University of Pittsburgh who dedicated their time to *Hot Metal Bridge*.

To the faculty, staff, and university.

To all the contributors we could not highlight.

Please visit our website and our incredible archive of writing at hotmetalbridge.org

Contents

Dear Reader

Hot Metal Bridge Editorial Team

Dear Reader,

"There it is, in your heart-shaped hands."
—Ayse Papatya Bucak ("I Cannot Explain My Heart")

Though these are the closing words for our special issue, they are a fitting place to begin as well. It's taken two decades of commitment and love of the written word to craft the collections that make up *Hot Metal Bridge*. Over the course of the last four months, in the midst of a global pandemic and ongoing injustices, a small group of graduate students came together to carefully review the legacy of *Hot Metal Bridge* and highlight some of the strongest writing to come out of it.

Founded in 2007 by MFA students at the University of Pittsburgh who wanted to create a space to spotlight emerging and established voices, *Hot Metal Bridge* is a graduate-student-led literary magazine dedicated to the discovery of good writing. Since its inception, *Hot Metal Bridge* has published several issues including fiction, nonfiction, and poetry. Featured in its pages, early work from writers like Sherrie Flick, Dan Chaon, Ewa Chrusciel, and Rodrigo Toscano, to name a few.

Best of Hot Metal Bridge

Named for a landmark spanning Pittsburgh's Monongahela River, *Hot Metal Bridge* connects new writers with renowned practioners of the written word.

As a collective, we returned to and nurtured our love of reading as well as the craft of storytelling during the global pandemic. Remembering, as one student shared, that "writing has truly been our bridge over troubled waters," we meditated and spent time in the tangle of emotions and circumstances of the average life in what is now the new normal. Engaging such feelings as desire, frustration, and being "washed in loneliness," as writer Tara Isabel Zambrano would phrase it, we committed to the task of fully embodying what it is to be human, celebrating our moments of triumph and evolution.

In honor of everything Hot Metal Bridge has accomplished in the last fifteen years, the current editorial team working on the journal have put together a "Best of" issue. We are thrilled to share it with you.

Before each selection, we have highlighted what we loved about it to warm you up before fully diving in. These creative essays, beautiful poems, and thoughtful tales cover themes that feel prescient today. This "Best of" issue, spanning topics of race, nationality, gender, sexuality, love, death, relationships, and more, encourages you to embrace the many fullnesses and truths of identity as well as celebrate your own.

With love,

Lorraine Avila, Kleaver Cruz, Lisette Escariz, K. Henderson, Willie Kinard III, Paola Liendo, Aeriel Merillat, Gabrielle Ralambo-Rajerison, Tanya Shirazi, and Amanda Tien

An Interview with Carolyn Kellogg

Hot Metal Bridge Editorial Team

Carolyn Kellogg is a writer and critic. She is the former Books editor of the *Los Angeles Times* and an award-winning culture writer. She is on the board of the National Book Critics Circle and has been published widely. She is also the founding editor of *Hot Metal Bridge*. We had the honor of getting an (extremely socially distant) email interview.

In this interview we discuss how *Hot Metal Bridge* came to be, the origins of its name, and what Carolyn Kellogg has been up to since graduating from the University of Pittsburgh's MFA program.

Q: Can you tell us a little bit about how you started *Hot Metal Bridge*? What inspired you to start a literary magazine at the University of Pittsburgh?

A: When I came to Pitt in 2006, the famed and beloved Chuck Kinder was running the program. Before our class of graduate students got to campus — I don't know if the subsequent directors have kept this up — he introduced us all to one another via email, and then before classes started had us all over to a party at his house. The way I remember it, it was at that party, where everyone was excited and a little buzzed, that he convinced us to start a literary magazine. It's possible it was a subsequent gathering with similar conditions — excitement, alcohol.

It's also possible he tricked us into thinking it was our idea.

Q: How did our journal get the name we all know and love—*Hot Metal Bridge*? Is there an origin story for how you landed on that name?

A: The name of the prior Pitt literary magazine had been Nidus, which, ugh. One of my colleagues came up with *Hot Metal Bridge*, and even those of us who were new to Pittsburgh thought it sounded great.

Q: What do you consider the biggest challenge in editing a journal? What about the biggest reward?

A: One of the biggest challenges editing the journal was just getting it off the ground. I'm so glad it's survived! The greatest reward was twofold: being able to ask wonderful writers if they'd contribute, tied with finding something terrific a new unknown writer had submitted.

Q: How did founding Hot Metal Bridge and your experience with the University of Pittsburgh MFA program shape your career?

A: Getting an MFA in fiction was important to me personally, and came at a time when I was moving from working in nonprofits into journalism. Being editor of *Hot Metal Bridge* gave me the opportunity to work closely with writers from other disciplines within the department, the poets and nonfiction writers, and with agency we didn't have in the classroom.

Q: You've had quite an impressive career, working at the *LA Times* as a staff writer and later the Books Editor and acting as one of the judges of the National Book Award in nonfiction. What has been your favorite project during this time?

A: Three things: Shortly after I became Books editor of the *Los Angeles Times* in 2016, I was able to create a group of Critics at Large — it was the only project of its kind at the paper — who wrote about books and also the current moment. I was so lucky to get these incredible writers on board: Rebecca Carroll, Alexander Chee, Rigoberto González, Marlon James, David Kipen, Laila Lalami, Adriana E. Ramírez, Viet Thanh Nguyen, John Scalzi and Susan Straight. I loved working with all of them.

Also, I spent a year working with the patient and indefatigable writer Melissa Chadburn on a story about literary hoaxster Anna March. It came out in the summer of the scammer, 2018, and I thought it was special because she was a member of the literary community. It was one of the paper's top 20 stories of the year and the presentation online was great https://www.latimes.com/projects/la-ca-jc-anna-march/

And judging the National Book Award was amazing. So many great books. The winner we selected was Sarah Broom's *The Yellow House* (read it!).

Q: What projects have you been working on recently that have brought you inspiration or hope?

A: I recently talked to Elizabeth Kolbert about her latest book, *Under a*

White Sky: The Nature of the Future (for a piece that's not yet published). For two decades Kolbert has been covering climate change for the *New Yorker*, and the news is universally terrible, but talking to her about where we are now inspired me to be increasingly cognizant of the choices I make, particularly in terms of energy consumption.

Q: What are you currently reading?

A: I just finished *Appropriate: A Provocation* by Paisley Rekdal, which is a careful and thorough examination of cultural appropriation, particularly in literature. It's great and goes much deeper than the high-pitched culture wars arguments that have made recent headlines.

Q: Book reviews are such an important part of the literary world and are something we hope to resuscitate in *HMB* in future issues. What has been your most memorable book review? Do you have any advice on how to shape book reviews?

A: One piece that's memorable for me was when I reviewed Thomas Pynchon's *Inherent Vice* for the *Los Angeles Times*. I was and am a huge Pynchon fan, and reading one of his books before almost everyone else and having the opportunity to have a definitive take on it was really a privilege. I got to work with a great editor, David L. Ulin, who made me promise to say the book was bad if it was and then trusted me. I think the book split Pynchon fans, which is fine; I personally thought it was a delight. I believe my lede made it onto the cover of the paperback: "'Inherent Vice' is Thomas Pynchon doing Raymond Chandler through a Jim Rockford looking glass, starring Cheech (or maybe Chong)."

Q: As an editor and book reviewer, what makes a piece of writing stand out to you?

A: An outstanding piece of writing almost always has a strong voice. Think of Lydia Millet's novel *The Children's Bible* or the essays of Tressie McMillan Cottom or reporting by Gustavo Arellano — very different voices, all creative and unique to themselves. Their thinking shines through.

Q: Lastly, do you have any advice for our community of emerging writers?

A: You've probably heard this one before, but read read read and write write write.

Skeletons

Hannah Soyer

["I am trying to write a fictionalized story about the terrors of change for the short story collection my friend and I are compiling but I don't know how to do this and so I simply tell the truth." This work tackles trauma headfirst in this piece. "Skeletons" announces itself: haunting and honest. — TS]

MONDAY: I am moving on Saturday. I am moving to a new town and new state which means I am leaving this town and this state and this home. I am moving and I am terrible at goodbyes. I am moving and I am trying to write a fictionalized story about the terrors of change for the short story collection my friend and I are compiling but I don't know how to do this and so I simply tell the truth.

I am packing in fits and spurts. One day I take out all of the boxes that a neighbor has lent me and space them out evenly over the living room floor. They are empty, for now.

When I sit down at my laptop between bouts of packing to type this I lay my hand flat on the keyboard and realize it looks dead, like something that doesn't belong to me, but instead a corpse found in the woods, the body of a girl abducted and betrayed and left for dead.

I am over two weeks late on my period - there is nothing growing inside of me*, though, only knots of stress. Perhaps my body is panicking at the thought of uprooting. Perhaps my body just doesn't know what to do.

**I read a story once about a girl who didn't get her period for an entire year after being raped because of the mental trauma. She finally asked her doctor about it at the end of the year, and when they sent her to the labs to have her blood drawn and tested for anemia, the lab technician couldn't even find a vein. They thought they did, after about 10 minutes of applying heat to her arms and massaging them, but once they stuck the needle in nothing came out. So she got sent to a specialist, who sent her to another specialist, who did the one thing all of the doctors should have done to begin with and tried to find her pulse. She didn't have one.*

TUESDAY: When I am not packing or trying to write I spend hours laying on the floor of my kitchen, staring up at the light above me. When I close my eyes the light doubles against my eyelids and I feel like I'm looking at one of those things you store your contacts in at the end of the day.

I don't know what to do about the skeletons in the closet. They don't fit neatly in any of the boxes unless I take them apart and I cannot do that.

My friends are coming at the end of the week to help me put all of the boxes and my couch into the moving truck and the skeletons must be put away securely by then, but I don't know how. When I go stand in front of the closet to look at them I am overcome by an abundant lack of answers. Sometimes I slide in between them and curl up in the darkness, letting their bones form a weird cloak around me. When I am pressed up against the back wall of the closet my mind is flooded with memories that make me bite my fist to keep from screaming in pain: the sight of tears running down my dad's cheeks at his friend's funeral, made blurry by my own tears, the sound my cat made when he was hit by a car, something too human, too close to a dying child, the smell of the room when I walked in on the man I was in love with on top of another woman, a sharp smell, a smell that cut my heart open and made me stumble and gasp no.

That man told me I was a masochist. The skeletons in the closet would agree with him.

WEDNESDAY: I am labeling each box* I pack, painstakingly arranging items so that their curves and points and edges fit perfectly together. *VERY FRAGILE KITCHEN* goes in black Sharpie on one - glasses I nicked from restaurants, bowls bought at goodwill, plates I took from my dad's house. Then there's *BOOKS* which has Michelle Tea and Maggie Nelson and Carmen Maria Machado, and *KNICKKNACKS* which has the cat statue and the pens and pencils and picture frames and jewelry and the collar from the cat. There's another kitchen box with half eaten food. And then there's my suitcase with clothes and another box of *HANGERS + BEDROOM DECORATIONS.* I am putting my travel-sized shampoo, deodorant, toothbrush and toothpaste in my backpack, along with my laptop and notebook. I have thrown out all of my makeup. Really, I can load all of these boxes into the truck myself. It's the couch I'll need help with. And then of course the skeletons are heavier than they look.

**I put pain in boxes, seal the boxes with tape, stack them in the closet.*

THURSDAY: The skeletons are not a metaphor. They're real. Real bone. Real human remains. I don't know how they got here, or maybe I do but don't want to tell. Or maybe my subconscious knows but my conscious does not. Maybe they were put in the closet* when I was gone some day or night or hour.

I wake up in the middle of the night to the sound of their bones knocking against the closet door.

**What if the skeletons end up being more alive than the person whose closet they're living is in? Like, the person who is actually made of flesh and blood and yes, bone, but also so much more than that. What if that person whose closet is home to a collection of skeletons - what if she's not actually powerful enough and by powerful enough I mean human enough and by human enough I mean woman enough - what if she can't make the skeletons leave?*

FRIDAY: I can't quite make myself take down the photos and posters from the walls. The feeling of an oncoming apocalypse has settled over me like a net. There is absolutely nothing I can do to stop tomorrow coming. Nothing at all.

Panic is lying low inside of me, a thin layer of pulsing fear far under my skin. But by midday it's merely an annoying distraction, and by evening, a quiet itch.

I put everything I can into boxes. When the only things left are my overnight backpack, mattress, and memories trapped in pictures on the wall, I open the door to the closet. The skulls are grinning at me. For one foolish second I think of leaving them, digging a hole in the park behind my apartment at night and bidding them good riddance. But of course this is impossible. I read a story once of a girl who buried her skeletons and before she had shoveled the last scoop of dirt onto their grave she had turned to stone.

So instead, I lay each skeleton on its back, one on top of the other, in a box I begged the co-op next door for. Their bones touch and make a sorrowful, hollow sound. Before I close the lid over them and tape it shut, I make myself stare into the black shadows where their eyes would be. A vision, then: Skeletons under my bed in my new apartment, skeletons peering around the door, skeletons crawling up to lay beside me and place their dead bone against my flesh. Acid rises, burning, in the back of my throat. I close the lid.

That night, I sleep in a room that is empty save for my mattress and posters on the wall.

SATURDAY: We are loading the boxes into the truck. What is harder to do - leaving a person or leaving a place?

The skeletons are quiet the whole time, even when their box gets jostled by the couch*.

I have the last box in my arms and suddenly the world is threatening to close in around me. The trees are losing their color, the grass seems to be turning brown, the pavement of the parking lot is churning. Run, I think. Run. Run. Run. My mind latches onto this word and I believe for a split second that this is a logical idea.

But of course there is the new apartment in the new city in the new state and the new job and new people. I hug my friends goodbye. I am climbing into the driver's seat of the truck, the last box beside me. I don't cry because I am still looking out at the world from behind the wall inside of me that's behind my eyes. I feel like I am choking but the only thing to do is drive.

I turn the key in the ignition and pull away from the curb. You will like this, I say to myself about the new apartment in the new city in the new state and the new job and new people, but the words bounce around in my skull and take on the tone of people from my past.

Even if the entire universe rearranged itself so that its star particles were ground particles and humans' cells made up the ocean, even if time stopped moving and showed up in a suit and tie and said "I'm quite tired now, I think I'll be done, may I have a cup of tea?" there are some things you can never stop from happening.

**I read a story once about a girl who took her skeletons with her when she moved because she had read a story once about a girl who had tried to bury her skeletons in the park but in shoveling dirt over their bones had turned to stone. The girl that took her skeletons with her couldn't find a big enough box to put them all in and so had to ask the undertaker - yes, I'm being serious - to use a box that he got coffins shipped to him in, and it turned out that that box worked. The skeletons, at least in the story, weren't happy about being put into a box that once held something that holds dead things.*

Woman

Qinglan Wan

[One editor shared her admiration for the writer's use of white space with black lines. "Woman" asks us to look very, very closely at the words we use to say anything and everything. — ajt]

"no whiteness (lost) is so white as the memory / of whiteness."
—Williams Carlos Williams, "The Descent"

Woman, female, other – haunt me. These words shape a cloud of faces. They glow and undulate, draw a border about me.

I am a tongue tucked within a body held in time, susceptible to the amorphous nature of language, and vulnerable to remembering: a space, whiteness, a personal re-construction.

The page looms in front me, as a block of white stands in place of my memory. Inhaling, the brush soaks in ink. Exhaling, the brush spreads black across white. A slow piecing of events, faces, and places eases the white into grey fog.

A meaning is captured and begins to be remembered. I define one word at a time, combing out the snarls of three languages that I have inherited. I start with Chinese. The tongue I was born out of. The tongue that I cling to.

nü, woman, she, female is a four-stroked character. Each intersection marks her compression. From the top, the line marks her head, an entry point. Pull the line down left and slide right. This is the first corner, where she shows her bound wrists. Outstretched from her body, the bound wrists create holes in her frame. Lift the brush. Move left to right. Slash the length of her chest. Reveal sloped neck and shoulder blades. The third corner on the right side appears. Mark her thighs, locked knees beneath the triangle of hips. Down the brush drops. This is the fourth and final corner, where her bound ankles sit. Faced down, she, an outstretched curve, does not see the writer tying her to the page.

女

It takes two lengths of rope to bind four human limbs together and render the body captive. It took one wrung out kitchen rag to tie my left wrist down to the leg of the dining table and one year for me to learn how to eat with my right hand. My Nagbu, maternal grandma, still gloats about this triumph. Since it is Chinese tradition to gather around a circular table for meals, I must learn the right ways of eating. One girl cannot disrupt the flow of meals and bring future shame to the family. I was a test from the heavens, sent to see if she could right the natural flow.

I stared at my full bowl, my right fingering the slippery chopsticks as my left crept up the teak leg and pushed my blue bowl closer to the edge. The left hand holds bowl below chin while the right pushes food into mouth. Every child must learn to eat with two sticks longer than her nose, must weld them as an extension of index and thumb. Tethered, I was a picky eater, not caring for wilted spinach or flakes of fish that slid off of chopsticks. Instead I speared sliced dark meat and grabbed buns with my fingers like a peasant.

To balance a grain of rice between two chopsticks is a display of refinement and breeding. *Balance is in everything*, repeated my mother over and over as she instructed me in calligraphy, after I was kicked out of the Chinese Learning Center. *It's all in the wrist.*

Her limpness pulled perfect wisps across the page. It was not my fault for knocking over the inkwell, I thought to myself. *It wasn't my fault. I didn't mean to.* It was more fun to grind ink than hold a thousand-haired brush. It was more fun to leave black handprints than to gently sweep the brush across rice paper. Two hands gripped my shoulder as the teacher gave me back to my mother. I was *a terrible girl, stubborn and unbecoming*. Her black bob bounced along, explaining my un-girlish behavior. Tight-lipped and apologetic, my mother took me back. *You need try harder to be a girl.* Every calligraphy lesson with my mother ended with my decisive throw of the brush against the page, bleeding the black ink into sheets of rice paper. Resolute in my resistance, I wrapped my arms around my knees and sulked in the corner until she left the room.

To stare at one grain of rice between two chopsticks is a waste of time. Years later, I learned to tuck in my elbows while holding a fork and knife over a plate. A land of sauce and vegetables bordered a slab of meat. I imagined falling face first into this plate-like map. Prostrated with elbows tucked in and knees crossed below a tented napkin, my body, a hinge of two opposing lines, becomes as simple as a woman.

父

fu, formal for father is a four-stroked hand
gripping a stick. Elongated, the black lines
pull into the profile of a man. Eyes
crinkled, the figure leans back. Hand raises
to stroke air. Force held in mid-strike. He
holds
out for honor, as it is his duty to dole
out strikes. He gains respect through
poised fear.

父

The word for parents in Chinese is 父母 (fumu: father-mother). The ordering of the characters depicting parents reflects Confucian tenet of filial piety, or 孝 (xiao), which is a sense of virtue and respect one holds for father, elders, and ancestors. Extrapolated further, filial piety defines a larger scale of cultural identity: father comes before mother, as husband stands before wife, man before woman, and sovereign before an individual.

Honor and fear make up a form that provides and strikes. It was not a stick my uncles used but the upturned black heel of a leather shoe. For the first three years of my life, I lived with my extended family while my parents worked abroad for two years. I turned three with the feel of rubber soles imprinted on the back of my thighs. I learned not to respect but to resent the scuff of heels as they entered the room. My legs reddened at my stubborn refusal to sit still, to be silent, to be good.

My earliest memory of my father is when he took me from Shanghai to Berlin in silence. He returned to fetch me because it was his duty. He, a tall stranger, pulled me through the air and dropped me onto a land of ashen white faces.

It was not a stick my father used but a leather belt that held his jeans to his waist. It first flew down onto my flailing back as I screamed and kicked at the apartment door. Cold air rushed at my face beneath the crack of door and floor. My mother stood off in the corner, waiting for my confusion to calm me, waiting for my father's tired anger to subside, waiting to gather my crumpled form into bed. Hiccupping, I promised these two strangers that I would be good if they let me go back.

A father runs the family unseen. He appeared only in bank statements, wads of cash on the kitchen table, and monthly stuffed animals. He was only overheard in arguments, where plates and chairs crashed into tables and tempers melted into fists, belts, and voices. Left behind are the crumbs of his distance. He is the one who faded first into the background, when my mother took me across two oceans, remarried, and started the turbulent cycle again for a third time.

A father is the silhouette trailing after me as I move forward from one place

to another. At times, he is just another man in the long line of men crossing my

path.

Sometimes I linger in conversations with him, in hopes he will grow familiar, benevolent, and comical. He is but a face that mirrors too closely to my own. No longer do I run away from the arc of lashes. I do not rise against the stance. I drop the pen and let him fade.

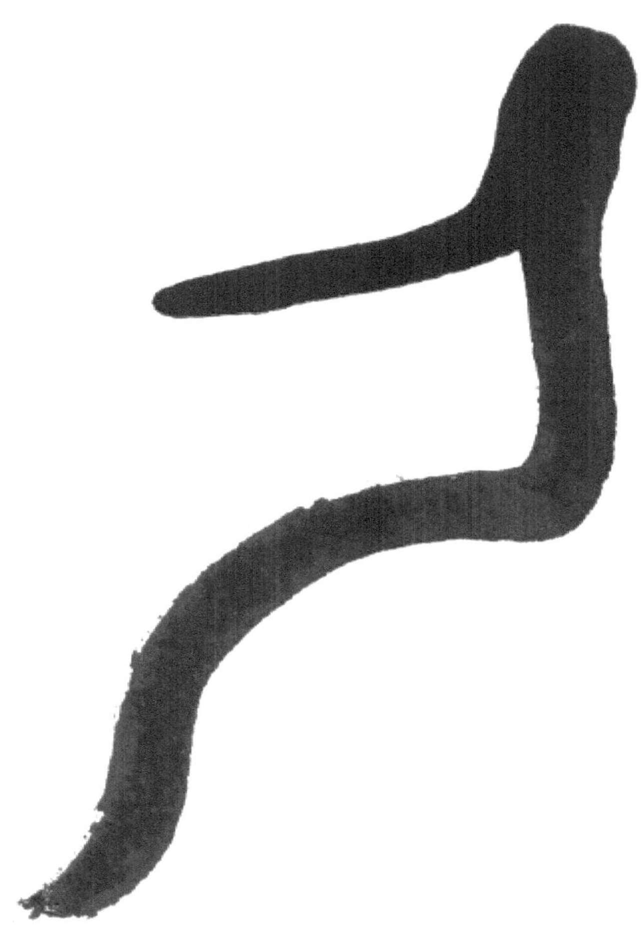

尸
shi, corpse
three-strokes outline the negative
space the body has left behind

母 (mu) formal for mother is a five-stroked character. Starting from top left corner, the brush pulls down and to the right, making the first bottom corner. This marks the pair of bound wrists. Lifting, the brush returns to the top left, crosses to the right, and drops down to complete the square. This right line goes past the first left corner, to mark her spine and her knees, seen in the small hook at the right-hand corner. The brush lifts again and drips the first of her two nipples, as signified in the top water drop. A line cuts across her chest. The second nipple is placed at the bottom, completing the character.

Without the two water-dropped nipples, the halved box resembles the character 毋 (wu), which means without, not, or nobody. To differentiate her from nobody, these two water drops show her anatomical difference. She is given personhood when offering her chest. Transformed from a bound shadow with holes, she reappears as a bound pair of breasts.

Personhood lies in a pair of bound breasts, procured, and offered. For the first four years of my childhood, I did not recognize my own mother. The year after I was born, my mother left Shanghai for Berlin to work abroad while my father went to Japan. My absent parents left me in the care of my grandparents and Amah, nanny. Without any real parents, I had every whim indulged. In my mother's eyes, this was the root my misbehaviors. She would first blame the heavens for cursing her with motherhood, chide me for my failures, and then claim I was the reason for holding her back in life.

She appears in halves, never as a whole. When my father returned to reunite the family in Berlin, my four-year-old self did not recognize these strangers as my parents. I was not the only one at a loss. My parents did not know how to care for me.

I grew silent and withdrawn, learning how to be alone in an empty apartment as my parents pulled long night shifts at the German Chinese restaurant. I learned how to be useful and cared for myself in their absence. As a child, I already understood that my parents were flawed human beings, lost in the darkness of their decisions.

She, the bound shadow, is the snake down my spine. My mother is a shadow, one I could detach from once I had found better replacements. One country after another, one year after another, it became easier to distance myself. I had the advantage of learning more about the new culture. She, a shadow, trailed behind me, bemoaning in Shanghai dialect her present predicament. An echo falling out of my ears, I held her off with German, then English. Later, I placed education and physical land between us.

To be without, to be a no-body is to see that I have become a woman without her.

The longer I stare at this character drying on this page, the less I see of my self. She, the breathing image of her self, is detached and separate from her body. A nebulous tense shadow remains bound to white. She rears her head only when my fingers trace the shallow grooves of my cheeks and dip down to the jut of my hips.

Qinglan Wan

In Memory of White Spaces

Stories are a truth told to define the past. Stroke by stroke, thick lines lengthen and narrow. I disappear to reappear in the repeated brushing of ink. Black changes white back into whiteness.

The imprint of an image captured in tiny scratches. A woman's body, once elongated over the page, compresses. She tightens to fit the confines of time. Torn apart, she is re-pieced anew. Repositioned, she is added to other radicals. One new meaning after another, time wraps a new layer over her. She becomes me. Yet the memory of her, a smudged shadow that once held a space on shells and bones, remains. White disappears in black and appears as white once more.

Us from Evil

Sally Rosen Kindred

[We were moved by this lyric exploration of grief as an embodiment of absence. How does absence have boundaries; take on dimension, shape? How does grief transform and transport us? In this poem, "Birth is recalled / by flight" as its assonance echoes forward, rhythm springs off the page, and familiar images become strange. — KEH]

Sorrow-skin womb, I refused you.
The airplane window forgives me.
Birth is recalled
by flight, its cry the speed required
to blur the earth. Glass sings
to me now about drowning. Sews a static shroud.

The airplane window is the reverse engineering
of the dead. Is the amnesiac tooth
of the moon.
Is how I forgot my own womb,
empty as the Afterlife and white
as the migraine dream that fills the plane.

While my body spills mud in the code.
While my hips chafe the belt,
ghosts and angels are free to move about the cabin.
See them rise and teach the floors to climb?
Down below, a shudder: the pilot light in the stove
of my first flesh house flares out.

Once, I had good knees.
My skin knew the prayer's liftoff verb, the one
my mouth had lost.
A mouth is an empty window, sometimes
intoning *deliver*. But not for you,
erased by thunderous light, all this bright machinery shaking:

my love, O vault of the never-born, your touch is a color
they don't make up here.
Look now: the aisle is a ladder.
The word I let go was *deliver*.
Saints of launch know how this light wounds through,
the burn changes the skin.

Godspeed, Boys

Zea Archer

[You know those songs that get stuck in your mind, and you keep looping over its sentences over and over again—an earworm? This essay felt like the nonfiction equivalent for me. There is something so fresh in the vulnerability of conception. It is personal and powerful. Upon review, we all immediately agreed it deserved a place in the "Best Of" collection. — ajt]

It's really just a glorified cervical cap. Insistently unsexy, it's a decided improvement on the penis which, I suppose, tries. It's meant for intravaginal insemination, which sounds like regular insemination because it is. With specimen cup locked in and plunger in place, semen is deposited at the terminus of the cervix and kept corked for up to six hours, after which it is neatly pulled out of the vaginal canal like a tampon. Its precision and functionality do take a lot of the spontaneity out of the attempt at conception—not to mention some of the fun. Evidently, the female orgasm is as integral to the process as its male counterpart—truly shocking—but "The Stork" isn't a sex toy. It's all work and no play, and we are in the business of getting pregnant.

*

After two years of talking about it, parenthood feels more like an inevitability than a possibility. Like something we are falling into. I wouldn't say we are careening, though at times it feels as fast. It feels more like diving. Falling with great purpose.

For a large chunk of whatever time it is normal to begin thinking about these things, I was certain I didn't want to be a parent. As difficult as it was for me to imagine myself as a mom, it was even more difficult to imagine myself as a partner, girlfriend, or wife. My distaste for parenthood was nurtured by my increasing and not wholly unwelcome belief that I would spend my life alone. It was generally understood that to be gay was to be single; maybe "partnered," but never "parent." Ellen didn't even have kids, for goodness' sake. Then, at twenty-one, I fell in love. Being in love can change a lot of things about a person. For me, it softened me in ways I so desperately needed to be softened. It changed my lens completely. The magic of falling in love cracked open possibility. Gay? Whatever. In love? Nothing is off limits. After getting hooked on a Youtube channel and reading a few illuminating books on the matter, my wife and I decided we were up to the challenge of disrupting the parenting paradigm. Good luck to us.

(To be fair, our desire for parenthood is in itself a disruption. To some, we're "playing God." To others, we're shamelessly conceding defeat to heteronormativity. Honestly, if someone is *asking* to spend the foreseeable future elbow-deep in feces and vomit, why stop them?)

In a fit of excitement, and with the loopy exhaustion of a visit to a black hole of internet reviews, I bought The Stork for my wife, for Christmas, one year ago. Since then, I've also bought: a basal body temperature thermometer, an ovulation tracking kit, six boxes of red raspberry leaf tea, and prenatal vitamins. For our donor, and dear friend: a fertility basket, including an at-home sperm test, male fertility vitamins, ashwagandha tea, a water bottle, essential oil diffuser, and checklist of "good foods and habits for fertility."

Will this confluence of conventional and natural wisdom procure for us a child? Will we conceive on the first try, or seventh, or at all? One gets the sense that we are somehow trying harder than most couples, though I know that isn't true. The stakes aren't any higher, nor are the chances any better. We are trying all the same, just with different tools.

For now, we are two months away from our first go at it—our first walk around the block while our friend ushers his raw genetic material into a cervical cap and leaves it on our kitchen counter; our first time loading the plunger, inserting, and releasing; our first time squealing with delight at the done deed, while I lay level with her midsection and imagine the cellular activity taking place; our first time waiting the perfunctory two weeks, while she feels every cramp and twitch like never before, both of us paying so much more attention to her body than anyone ought to their own; the first pregnancy test, or first disappointing period; and first time waiting two weeks to try it all again. Our donor is confident it will be one-and-done, but he has more confidence in his reproductive abilities than I do in mine. While a majority of the reviews bubble and exclaim about The Stork delivering on the first attempt, I can't help but temper my expectations. I'm putting my faith—my future—in a non-reusable applicator device, a piece of $59.99 plastic on the shelf at CVS.

*

What will it mean to help someone conceive? I am filling a space rarely occupied—a third person in the room in which sperm and ovum meet. I will be the vessel through which the seed of life bursts open. I will carry the specimen cup with holy reverence up the stairs of our century-old colonial and prostrate before the life-giving altar, a supine woman on a bed. I will gently guide the applicator through a reverse trip into the birth canal, and I will plunge the petals open and deliver to the mighty cervix an offering, tens of millions of offerings. I will say a blessing as the journey commences and my work as interlocutor concludes: *godspeed, boys.*

This is the origin story of so many lives, and yet so few, and still entirely its own. Who am I to the life begun here? A middle man? Technically unnecessary? Just a big kid playing God with sperm and egg?—dare I say: a parent?

As the great work begins—in a uterine tube, in the body of a woman I love, maybe while sleeping, or running, or on an airplane—I will be ready for the labor. Used to plunging—feet first, cap erect, and with abandon—I will dive into this new life. If I was good enough to be God for a moment, I'll be good enough for whatever is next.

Alight

Sally Wen Mao

—after the installation "Derelict," Hema Upadhyay

The arsonist in me salivates
when I see the chandelier made of matches
hanging from the hook at the Mattress

Factory. I imagine a flame kissing
its thousands of red charred nipples,
seeing the museum, the chairs, ignite.

Then I imagine whole villages
made of matches; a flammable city
where lovers drink cold tea

in bed, setting off smoke alarms
and fucking as the lights go out,
and every drop of sweat

could light on fire: even the dew
on tulip bulbs trembles in heat

with stamens that tease.

I imagine a shirtwaist factory,
vanishing, releasing balloons
into the roseate air; a slime trail,

a fire slug, hydrants erected
on every lawn, men soaking rags
in steaming water, the smell of oleanders

tart & smoke-seared. Then the kerosene.
Skinny, soot-kneed, it is a girl. She opens
her lungs, unpeels the poultice.

Once You've Gone Back Home

David E. Yee

[We loved this piece for its thoughtful exploration of the friendships that both stain and sustain us. "It's really simple, isn't it?" one character asks another. "But there's something wounding to it." — GRR]

They'd gathered to watch Hao sing—his first public performance. There'd been fractions of rehearsals, drunk nights in a dim living room, a few songs to end the night after the beer ran out, but never a stage. I only went to get more time with Tulsa, and sat next to her at the back counter, looking at Hao through the beer taps. A Stratocaster belted to his skinny-jeaned hips. His neck craned to the low microphone. Fresnel lights thumbed a shadow across his long face. Six-string chord changes droning under his Johnny Cash drawl, he sang slow enough to rake you with confessional lyrics, always a clever turn in the refrain, and that was the difference between us, I didn't know how to be clever. We'd come up in a garage band together, playing little basement shows and bar gigs for free drinks. That trailed off sometime before he and Tulsa started dating. Then it was all smiles and *Hey sweetheart*, never one without the other. Their comfort—boothed across from it in restaurants, elbow-to-elbow with it in bars, how they communicated in glances as if words were an afterthought—had been an eighteen-month sprained ankle for me, a nagging reminder that I was unfamiliar with that ease.

Or maybe I was just jealous of him. We'd been something like inseparable once—those friends who often bickered until stumbling on an old joke and silently forgiving each other. He used to call me a brute cause I'm the stocky sort of Chinese. My mother said our people belonged on the water—thick-necked and short-limbed, dark skin begging for sun—that it takes a specific strength to drag the nets against the tide. Told me this when I got expelled from the ninth grade in Cambridge for fighting. I was heading to Fenwick to live in my aunt's trailer on the coast, just south of the state line. I'd been there ever since. My aunt passed a couple years back. I remember thinking, *Well that's something*, while I gripped the new deed to her place, my name adrift in the lines of bold print.

Hao lived two docks over, separated by the bay's green fingers. When we met, I was convinced we'd always be the odd men out and day dreamed about heading west to DC, or up to NY where being Asian wasn't something of note. He was hesitant to believe it, said I was just imagining myself as an outsider. There was German in his blood—he was taller, fairer, made friends easily. As teens, we'd leave his stuffy trailer after band practice and lie on the docks, smoking my aunt's Virginia Slims. Sometimes, she'd sit with us while we talked about the songs we'd never write. She didn't care if we drank her liquor, and two pints of MD 20/20 in, Hao said when he was a kid, he used to think the chirps of the crickets were the stars whistling, trying to get his attention. He raised his arm toward the sky, pretending to pinch one faint glow between his thumb and forefinger. I yanked the bottle from his other hand, said, *Someone's had enough*. The chalky liquid churned in the bottle, and my aunt smiled, told me not to be jealous and left her cigarettes on the foldout chair.

Now, in the bar, Hao began a song about his first love—a girl from Philadelphia. She'd just graduated, had come to the beach for vacation. Her inevitable return home made them move quick, and at that pace, they found something like meaning. Hao said, *She left for home and my home was here, in the scene of that momentary obsession*. Tulsa asked me what she'd been like, and I said she was pretty—*real pretty*—the kind that lingers. The way Hao went about singing it, with contempt for his younger self, all of those summers before we turned twenty-one seemed foreign.

We'd been lifeguards since eighteen, used to walk home from the beach, passing a water bottle full of vodka between us, wondering whether we'd ever get tired of the tourist months. We figured we would but hoped against it. The sun rubbed light on the hem where the sky sank into the bay, the distant thump of hip hop in motel rooms lining the road. I threw my arm over Hao's shoulder while three girls and a dude came the opposite way. The guy said, Hey where's the party? Their bathing suits were still waterlogged and dusted with sand. I raised the bottle toward his face, and he smelled the rubbing alcohol scent of the Rikaloff, said, *Oh shit*. Hao said, *Help yourself.* They followed us to a good strip of beach north of the boardwalk, one where businesses didn't shine their patio lights out toward the ocean. We sat in the dark on our towels and played Sip-Sip-Pass until the vodka ran out.

There's nothing like the ocean at night—the break of the waves unfettered by gull calls or the crowds conversing. Hao showed the girls the stick-and-poke tattoo of a mallard he'd stitched onto his bicep. They circled around him, asked him how he did it, and he recreated the process with a barb of driftwood for a needle, a palm of water as India ink. I stood, joints loose from the booze, in the wet sand with the foam of the wake lapping at my feet. A chill breeze rushed past, and I felt like I was standing on the lip of a mouth, the slow exhales of something giant. I knew how quickly the ocean could eat you. That fear of fragility—of being swallowed up against my will—had burned like fuel in me, was what made me say *Yes* in the face of self-doubt. I figured I spent too much time in the Atlantic, that one day the water would catch me off-guard, and I'd be damned if I didn't live a life before it got me.

We're twenty-six now, and I still get that fist-tightening excitement when summer begins. Route 1 steadily swelling with packs of sandal-wearing families, a herd of college kids, new faces rushing toward the breaking waves. Every week a shuffling of the cards, and Hao and me, we'd been there all along.

*

Tulsa changed that rhythm. Nights when we'd go to the busier bars down near the single digits, she'd tag along, and then there was no more flirting with vacationers. I used to tell people I only lived there for the summer. At a club, I got a number, and Tulsa leaned against the counter, said, *Who wouldn't want to call the beach home?* She didn't understand. These people didn't need to know that when they left for the winter, I went back to chasing shifts at the bar, to off-season work scrubbing empty hotel pools, the cleaner eating my cuticles. Few years back, Hao started teaching guitar up in Rehoboth. He was making steady money, year-round work. And with Tulsa waiting for him after his lessons, he stopped grabbing the bus with me downtown.

Shit changed with our friends when he was absent. That first question as I sidled up to the circle—*Hey, where's Hao?*—annoyed the shit out of me. Still, I was relieved to be away from their coupling. I downed beer after beer with this image of them splitting Hao's beat-up leather couch, building a private life up like walls around each other. They didn't need me. And yet, they were not unkind, inviting me over a couple times a month to listen to records while Hao cooked. I'd bring a six-pack and drank my two as Tulsa asked me about us as boys. I said, *We were the kids you wanted to know. You remember Sharkey's, man? Hao's sister used to date the bartender there, never carded us.*

Hao was chopping onions, took a break to sip his beer, saying, *Shit, whatever happened to Marcus? I haven't seen him since that place shut down.* The belly of the trailer filled with the salt-thick scent of fat cooking off flank steak. I said, *How many boardwalk girls you think gave us the time of day just cause we knew a spot to drink?* Hao's face went flush, a chuckle low in his throat as he stared into the pan, stirring the vegetables into the meat. Tulsa reached over and mussed his hair, said, *Well it certainly wasn't for your looks.* We talked into the night until the conversation became riddled with quiet gaps—a signal I'd come to understand as a marker for my exit, allowing them to return to that thing they could only occupy alone.

*

Just after Labor Day last year, Hao's car broke down, and he asked me to take him to work. I was done on the beach for the season, had the afternoons off, so we hopped in my aunt's pickup and headed north. He said, *What're you doing for work now? You going back to Rusty's?* Told him I'd gotten a job serving at a crab house, bayside. It did good business, even in the winter. He nodded, slowly, like he wasn't quite hearing me. The day was overcast, gray clouds blending into the pitch water visible through dips in the sand dunes. Hao's black hair was tipped with grease. I knew he'd been skipping the shower. When we were younger, we'd go a week without anything but ocean water and a quick rinse in the outdoor faucets stationed on the beach. The salt made our thick hair wavy and malleable, our skin dark and taut. We were creatures born of the sea. He looked out at the dunes, said, *You think you can get me some shifts?* I asked him if everything was alright, if he still had guitar students, and he said, *Yeah, yeah. Of course. I'm just trying to stay busy.*

No one could tell me why they'd ended it, but it had gotten around that they weren't dating. I'd be lying if I said that didn't well up some excitement in me. Worked out we fell back into our old habits without her—drinking till close at the bars we knew, talking about back in the day. I showed him some songs I'd been working on, and he did the same. It was clear how much better he'd gotten over the years with steady practice. I had to be bored to even pick up my SG. We spent more time with music, even talked about starting up a band again, and he said he'd think about it just as soon as he got his record done. He'd been trying to finish for years.

*

Tulsa talked to each and every person she met as if they were, in that moment, the most important being on her planet. It wasn't a surprise when our friends tacitly decided that she'd remain one of us—a group she could count on to gather at the beach near 130th, who'd invite her to family dinner every Monday and Industry night at Rusty's on Sunday. Tulsa hadn't come up in Ocean City like the rest of us, didn't know how to keep going in the cold months when the population dropped and the very blood of Coastal Highway slowed to a halt. You need to have people to help make it through the winter.

But the people belonged to Hao. The audience huddled around him like warmth, the half-full room congested in front of the stage, set apart from the scuffed dance floor by a riser. They clapped with each interval in the music, singing lyrics when they knew them. There was nothing flashy to his performance, nothing anyone hadn't heard before, and yet Hao had a way of twisting that familiarity to be heartfelt. I leaned over to Tulsa, said, *It's really simple, isn't it? But there's something wounding to it.* She hadn't looked at me since the set started. She said, *He's entirely honest up there.*

It happened, at first, unconsciously, that I wanted to elevate her in the way she raised others. That position was unfamiliar to me, and in its strangeness, I became absorbed in how the world I came up in *took* to her. The nights I wasn't serving, when I'd ask Hao to go to the bar and he'd turn me down to record, when I would end up going by myself, searching for easy company, I started inviting her along instead. Told myself I was just being a decent friend, a good person. Maybe that was true—if nothing else, it showed I hadn't just been her friend because she was dating Hao, that she was worth knowing. And yet, I am not a good person, have never really claimed that moniker. I'd always found that if I was honest with myself about what I wanted, those desires interfered with my friends' lives—couldn't work there because they fired this person, couldn't date her because so-and-so has a crush, can't play in that band because so-and-so got kicked out of it. It didn't matter if I acted on them. The urge itself condemned me. So it was unsurprising that I wanted to be in Tulsa's presence—her licorice black hair, those blue eyes, the way she burped halfway through a beer. I wanted to be the one she exhaled around, outside the view of the world I knew.

We discovered a mutual love for pool, had a weekly game at the Sand Dollar where the drinks were cheap and the felt of the tables was red. Few years ago, she'd followed some skateboarder here from Baltimore. The plan was that he'd use the off-season months to practice, to shoot a promo video, then they could party through the summer. When he bailed, she got stuck with the lease, and by the time it ended, she'd found a paying job at a preschool and her coworker had set her up with Hao. We're shooting pool one night, and I was curious, so I nagged her about why she'd ended it, and she said, *It was mutual. He's got such a decent heart in him, but that's not always enough.*

That didn't satiate me, didn't explain this fault in them that I had missed. I let her win a few games, bought the next round. Asked her again, saying, *Come on, it's just me.* Her expression looked more exhausted than trusting, but trust is a form of giving in. She said, *Hao is good. He's talented and beautiful and good. We wanted it to work, but like, you can only spend so much time thinking everything would make sense eventually, you know?* She paused to make the five in the corner, scratching the cue, saying, *We weren't happy.* I could sense her spirit folding as she said it, surrendering to those three words, and I didn't mean to take her there. I raised my drink off the end table after I missed a glancing shot, said, *Well, now you're stuck with the rest of us lowlifes.*

At pool, we'd kept a running record. The day of the show, I was up 58-41, but we hadn't played in a few months. When summer started, I got a call from my mother. My sister had been in a car wreck. I locked up the trailer, spent the hot months with my family in Minnesota while she recovered. Didn't think it would be right to leave before she could walk, and weeks slipped away before she could even sit up. In August, she swiveled in her bed and stood barefoot on the sterilized tile. My mother hadn't touched her while she was bedridden, even when the nurses said some contact was fine. She wore her wool sweater and slacks loose on her rail-like limbs, wringing her hands together instead of clearing sweat from her daughter's forehead or adjusting the part in her mocha hair, all for fear of worsening the damage. She'd always been like that, thinking she only made things worse. My sister, standing, reached for my mother, and they grasped each other's shoulders, knees shaking, fingernails digging. My older brother in the corner of the room, shouted, *I told you! I told you!* Over and over and I ached for him to stop, his words cutting ribbons out of this reunion. In the hallway, I said, *You always do that shit. You always involve yourself in other people's moments.*

I'd gotten that news in a voicemail while at work. My phone was dead, so I didn't see it until I'd had my shift beers and got to the charger in my car. Mom had caught the last flight out of BWI and booked me the only seat to Minneapolis the following day at three. I could've gotten a ride from almost anyone, but Tulsa and I were supposed to shoot pool that night, thought that was reason enough to ask her. It was two AM, and my call woke her. Told her about the accident, about the spinal contusion and the numbness in my little sister's limbs, how she couldn't support her own weight. She was a freshman at UM, the passenger in a car on the way home from a party. Driver didn't make it. Tulsa said, *I didn't even know you had a sister.*

What can I do? I said, *I need a ride to the airport tomorrow.* My voice felt disconnected from my lungs as I spoke—worry for my sister made my heartbeat rap on my esophagus, yet part of me was still looking for an excuse to see her.

Tulsa showed up at my place too early, my flight was hours away. She knocked on the trailer window to wake me. I let her in and she examined what I'd thrown on my duffle bag—board shorts, a few T-shirts, the entirety of my clean underwear. She said, *Have you ever been to Minneapolis? You need to pack some pants, maybe a sweatshirt.* I did as I was told, and then it was just me and my packed bag, nine in the morning. She looked at me as if I were a stray limping out of the wilderness, hungry for compassion. She said to *come on*, that she was going to take me somewhere, then carried my luggage to her Civic. The bright red paint on her car used to annoy me when I started toward Hao's, knowing she would be there. As we pulled out of the cul-de-sac, I couldn't bring myself to glance over but could still see, in my mind, the maroon trellises lashed to the side of his trailer, the plastic awning yellowed by the rain.

Route 50 turned north before I asked her where we were going. She said, *You just find an appetite.* We spoke about my sister's health until every answer became *I don't know*, and then she talked idly about her job, about gossip, things she'd heard around the way. She said, *So you're seeing Tina from Rusty's? She's pretty.* I shook my head, said we'd gone out a couple times, but it wasn't right. The road toward the Bay Bridge felt like it was sinking beneath the rain-thick grass, as if the flat fields were soft enough to swallow up the cement. *So you're more of a boob guy?* she posted her left hand atop the wheel, right elbow on the middle console.

I coughed out a laugh, said, *It's not like that.* Tulsa perched her chin atop her fist, head turned my way, eyes slipping from the road ahead. She said, *I'd kill for her legs.* I took it as an invitation to think of her lower half, a tattoo of an eagle shot full of arrows astride her right thigh, the scar from a bike accident on her left shin. I liked the way she crossed her legs at the ankle as she applied tanning oil, standing beside her beach towel, her back to the sun.

At the ascension of the bridge where the Jersey walls gave way to pale steel barricades, the road cleared the Chesapeake and climbed into the wet air. Tulsa rolled the windows down, the wind whipping her hair about her face. She let her left hand glide out the window—a flesh kite in the current—yelling over the roar of air racing into the car, *This thing scares the piss out of me.* She flinched, pulling her lips back, not in a smile, but a taut line, the uncomfortable expression of someone expecting pain. In the middle of the ten-minute bridge, under the framework where the barricades rise to a point out of view, it's easy to feel a caged sort of safety from the green water a hundred feet down. But on the incline, the decline, the barriers are just low enough to see the danger below. As a kid, shuttled across it, I felt no fear, convinced that no man made structure built allowed harm to those inside it. Looking over the side now, the girders throwing shadows across the red paint of the hood, I thought about when that semi struck a car last year, sent it plunging into the water. How that woman survived, I wasn't sure. I knew if it were me, I wouldn't be so lucky.

Tulsa pulled into a strip mall twenty minutes south of the airport, took the keys from the ignition, said, *Hao ever bring you here?* I shook my head, unfamiliar with the sandstone building, the cyan paint along the roof chipped and faded. The corner Chinese restaurant had a paper sign under the hours that read *Dim Sum Every Weekend.* My mother had taken the family to Dim Sum when I was younger, and I remembered, fondly, the draping smell of meat and oil, the pristine tablecloths, waiters pushing carts of metal steaming dishes that rattled as the wheel caught a lip in the carpet. I poured her tea and we pointed at the buds of shumai, shrimp dumplings, pork buns and taro pudding. The waiter stamped our ticket, piling the dishes onto our two-top. I shoveled rice into my mouth, said, I never realized how much I missed this. She had a cheek-full of garlic greens, a bit of sauce staining her lip. Another cart came and I shook my head at the tripe and the chicken feet, but Tulsa said we'd have both. She said, *What? You're too good for scraps?* She plucked two of the clawed feet from the bowl of broth, holding them above the table and walking them over to my plate as if the bird itself was above the cooked appendages. I looked at the orange limbs, greasy and lifeless, said they were gross. When she spoke, Tulsa looked almost embarrassed, saying, *They're for your sister. It's a silly thought, I know. Feet for her feet.* She glanced at the white table linen for a moment, and I nudged her shoe with mine, saying, *Thank you.* We ate every appendage to the marrow.

*

Two beers into the set, Hao played a slowed version of "Freak Scene" by Dinosaur Jr.—one of my favorite songs. We used to blast it in the trailer, headbanging on the couch until my aunt got off work. *Didn't realize he liked this song that much,* I said. I tapped my heel on the footrest, annoyed at how the lyrics still made my hair stand on end, that it was his mouth delivering them. When he got to the last verse, he lifted his head from the crowd, looked me directly in the eye. I couldn't tell if he was smiling, but I raised my glass off the bar toward him and he turned back to the microphone. Watching his forearm pulse above the guitar, pinched fingers strumming the gap above the pick-up, I would be lying if I said I didn't want to be there next to him, playing the root chords, letting him embellish the melody, the solo.

When I got back to Ocean City, I called Tulsa to see if she was up for a night at the Sand Dollar, to catch-up, and she asked if I was free that afternoon, said she needed to borrow the truck. I drove her up to Rehoboth to pick up a new mattress. Her last one was her ex's and she was tired of how soft it was in the middle, tired of waking up with a sore back. We were walking through the aisles of the furniture store as she pressed her palm into the springs of each cushion. *Plus*, she said, *There's a lot of old boy sweat in mine. I'm ready for a clean break.* The thought of Hao's condensation in her sheets made me cringe, and the souring on my face made her laugh. I was not unaware that the two of us testing mattresses on Saturday afternoon resembled a couple. She said, *I need something that is firm enough to sleep on my stomach, but soft enough to spend the occasional day nesting in.* I asked what that felt like, and she said she'd know it when she found it. She kept politely shooing sales attendants, eventually found herself stationed on a full-sized pillow-top in the window of the store. I was on my phone, texting people that I was back in town, and *We should hangout sometime*, watching her bounce on the foot of the bed, her lower back peaking out over her shorts. She collapsed onto it, looked at me from flat on her back, saying, *Come here*. I would be lying if I said that I didn't imagine, right then, what it would be like to fall asleep beside her, to feel her forehead, sweat-slicked, against mine, an hour of sex behind us—thinking *Fuck you, Hao*. Seated on the bare mattress, she said, *What do you think?* I pressed a hand into it, the springs below the top cushion barely gave. *It's firm*, I said. She grabbed a fistful of my shirt, fingers grazing my spine, pulled me alongside her. See? It's good right? The ceiling tiles above us were ringed with brown water stains. I could feel her breath churning in the upholstery.

I strapped it to the bed of my pickup, helped her carry it into her home. I'd never been in her room before, was surprised at how bare the walls were, her dresser drawers unclosed and bulging with clothing. By that time, I'd gotten a couple texts about the show, but I didn't mention it until she said, *You know Hao is playing tonight, right?* I nodded, seated on the bare mattress again, watching her rifle through shirts in the closet. I said, *You going?* She got to the last hanger, saying, *I should really do laundry. Or clean up a bit.* I shrugged, *I think you look good.* The springs had so little give as she sat down beside me. Rubbing her palms in her lap, she said, *He stopped practicing while we were together. I feel like he wouldn't want me there. I slowed him down.* When I wrapped my arm about her and touched her on her side, I wanted to will him from her mind, to reassure her, not that he wouldn't care, but that for as much as he might not want her around, I did. I said, *I'll go if you go.*

*

Hao's black hair was brimmed with sweat, the collar of his shirt flattened by the guitar strap. He looked wet and pink, as if he'd just come in from a run, and yet, basking in the attention of the audience, he belonged nowhere else. He said, *This last song is a slow one. Not that any of my stuff is that upbeat.* The crowd chuckled as he took the capo from the headstock and locked it to a fret, saying, *It's called "Last Song for Sweetheart."*

I couldn't tell you the words, just that the chorus lyric was the title phrase repeated twice, paced the first time and even slower the second. Hao's left hand dragging down three notes in a scale, his vocal following in harmony—I caught the look on Tulsa's face as he sang it, how she felt every word as if the notes themselves had hooks that flew from the amplifier, snagging her eyelids, her rouged cheek, the very curve of her lips. Twitches like microscopic explosions rippled through her expression, and I knew it as the face of surrender, of recognizing a love you once called home and all the ways it was given up.

Leaning into the bar, I could feel in my chest—was so sure—that I lacked those same barbs to harm her, that I could never eclipse the affection she'd already had, that love she wanted but not enough. I prepared myself for a crippling sort of failure at this, of loss or embarrassment, but found myself beholden to their faces as the song played on. To witness their mutual beauty, to know the circumference of what they meant to each other, and yet to be apart from it, still warmed me like hands over an exposed flame. Long after I moved away from the coast, after I gave up music all together, I find myself rehearsing that moment when they stepped briefly back into that world they built together—how it was there to come back to. It makes for a nice foundation to live upon—a center to raise my walls around, to house my unstill heart, and wait. The song ended, and she teemed with grief. The blue in her irises laminated with a near invisible sheen, and yet, Tulsa smiled. Without taking her eyes from him, she whispered, *That's what's different. He wants everything painful to be pretty.*

The Sixth Arrondissement

Alejandro Escude

[We were struck by the startling turn of this poem's images, which guide us through a meditation on idealism, cultural imagination, romance, and romanticization. Can we love anything for what it truly is? Can we love anyone for who they truly are? — KEH]

She degrades. The candles wrap themselves
Around the candle night the candle moon.
I will the end of the video woman.
You will recall the quiet between the reeds
In the sixth arrondissement. You took my hand
And we prayed in that non-church.
I sit at my non-church making verses.
My sunglasses are awake. They will outlive us.
There are some days that go by without news of the sun.
I watched you put your hair in a bun.
Satchels went un-snatched. Thieves starved.
Every other nightclub is full of the unborn.
No one lights a cigarette anymore.
Even the man in the corner balcony lights up
Like a scientist studying the effects of tobacco.
The world is against Putin. Putin the world hates you.

They say the head on Castro's latest picture
Was airbrushed in. Just an old head.
Castro meeting with Clinton. In Cuba,
The ocean reeks of seaweed and rusty cars.
There's a Lucille Ball in every bar.
Every government is in some way a farce.
Watch for Ricky's hand Lucy, he loves you but...
It's happening now. In some lonely hotel room.
Leonardo DiCaprio takes a picture of himself
With his phone, standing on bleachers
As I did in middle school to sing our graduation song.
Lean on me, Lean on me, When you need a friend...
Who knew life would come down to two
Conversations; one on Catalina Island,
In a little cove, my wife said, yes, I will marry you,
And the other, in bed, the sun coming up.

Men are not Mirrors

Caroline Cabrera

["Not all scars/are permanent," is the balm of the story Cabrera illustrates over the course of this reflection on navigating a world with men who attempt to assert their desires and lustful wishes on the poem's speaker and other bodies like theirs. — KC]

There is the movement I make and the shadow
of that movement and the memory of movement
which stays in the room for a while like lights-gone-off
burned into the backs of your eyelids. Not all scars
are permanent. Maybe I am walking at a pace
that makes me invisible to you. Maybe I have fixed
my hair a few times. For work I dress chin to ankle
and still my body can be too much. Still the old man
at the supermarket insists on bringing our cart out
so he can encourage me to get pregnant. He says,
sometimes you go to sleep at night and then wake up pregnant.
Sometimes we have met somewhere in two separate
cars and we must drive home separately so I cannot
keep telling you what I heard on the radio. And anyway,
we hear new things. Your body moves through the world
and my body moves through an entirely different
world, though we can see each other mostly the entire time.

Hiding Places

Pablo Piñero Stillmann

[Even though this piece was published in 2017, its themes hit different in 2020: nationality, fake news, the sense of disembodiment with video calls, elections. This short story gave us international spy vibes plus domestic debate, anchoring in the question: "Is my mother a liar?" (The answer is, as it is for all human beings, yes.) — ajt]

I wasn't on speaking terms with my mother when she left for Egypt to chase an ex- boyfriend. That Saturday I woke up to a series of her texts:

Boarding [plane emoji] to Paris then Cairo. 12:57AM

Please look after the house&Goyo. 1:01AM

[Three money bags emoji] in envelope in freezer for expenses. 1:03AM

(I'd once told her of an American congressman who was caught with $100,000 stashed in his freezer. She was delighted by the story and often found excuses to imitate the disgraced politician.)

Annoyed, I immediately called Juan Carlos, as my mother was by then somewhere over the Atlantic.

"What?" I'd woken him up.

"How about *hello*?" I said.

My brother works 65-hour weeks and then attempts to sleep through the weekend.

"What do you want, Antonio?"

"Mom left for Egypt?"

"And?"

"Why Egypt?"

"That's why you called me?"

"She texted saying I was in charge of the house and the dog."

"And?"

"What about Guirnalda?" I said. "Doesn't she usually take care of things when Mom's gone?"

"She's pregnant. Left three months ago. Goodbye."

"Wait! I just don't understand how she just—"

"I'm sleeping."

"Do you know when she's coming back?"

"No."

Click.

The key was in its usual hiding place: inside a fake avocado hanging from the tree outside my mother's house. (It wasn't even an avocado tree, but that had never been a problem.) Goyo did his darndest to wag his tail as I entered. The big guy always liked me. Enjoying his company would be one of the perks of this arrangement. Another one would be living in a big house with a beautiful garden out in the calm suburbs instead of in a tiny, old apartment surrounded by noisy neighbors and a bustling neighborhood. The downside—

The downside is hard to explain. Let's just say I didn't have a happy childhood. Let's also just say that when my father left our lives turned chaotic. The house, and I've never completely understood this, always provided me with a sense of calm but also deep sadness. It was a bit as if your favorite warm blanket gave you cancer. If the house could've talked, it would've said something like, *Everything's alright for now, but just you wait…*

I tried to focus on the positive. The garden, for example, looked gorgeous under the morning sun. I left my travel bag in my childhood bedroom and went outside to one of the reclining chairs with the latest issue of *The Economist*. Sonia called me soon after.

"We got him by his tiny balls," she said. "His tiny, wrinkled, hairy balls."

"What are you talking about?"

"Of all your faults, Toño, your biggest is probably that you're too out of it. Turn on a goddamn laptop, an iPad. Hell, turn on a fucking TV."

Sonia, my boss, was a barely thirty, super successful workaholic. For her, Saturday was just a weekday with less traffic.

"Laptop open," I said from inside the house.

"Go to *El Universal*."

There was a picture of a high-rise right next to the ocean. Under it, the headline read: *Navarrete Owns Six Luxury Properties, Two in Miami.*

"You don't need to read the article," said Sonia. "Just get to work. Two weeks until the election. *We need all hands on deck*." She said this last phrase in English before hanging up. Sonia loved peppering her conversations with English phrases as a way to remind people that she did a semester of college in Austin, Texas.

Back when I was a political science student, all I wanted was to work for a big consulting firm and get urgent phone calls. After graduation, and almost a year of unemployment, one of my ex-classmates, who knew I wasn't having much luck in the Real World, told me Soto Consultores was looking for people to join their team.

I sent my CV to SC's HR and, excited, read up more about them on their website. Their offices were in the upper floors of a new, gargantuan building overlooking Chapultepec Park. I began to imagine myself walking into that building in a suit and tie while talking on the phone with a client.

HR called only a couple of hours after I sent the email and told me a little, very little, about the job. Then we set a date for a Skype interview with Sonia. The interview went well and she offered me the job before we said goodbye.

Working for SC, however, turned out to be nothing like what I'd imagined. For starters, after almost two years at the firm I'd never even visited their offices. I'd offered several times to attend in person, but Sonia would always say something like, *Why bother?*, or, *It's already so crowded in here*. My work uniform, instead of a designer suit, consisted of flip-flops, pajama pants and a tattered Centre Pompidou sweatshirt my mother bought me years ago on a trip to Paris. (For Skype sessions with Sonia, I'd tuck in a button-down into my pajama pants and comb my messy hair.)

While my formal job title was Opposition Research and Special Events Monitoring Executive, I was mostly just a digital goon. My main duty was to come up with memes, tweets and other social media content and disinformation to slander our clients' opponents. This content would then be deployed by the infinite number of bots and official-looking websites created and managed by SC's IT guys. My finest work had been during the Coahuila gubernatorial campaign. One of our opponents was rumored to be in business with a cartel leader. Using a picture of the candidate in a bathing suit, I photoshopped a tiny head of the cartel leader coming out of his shoulder with the caption, *THIS FUCKING TUMOR IS KILLING ME*. It was a rush job and I didn't think much of it at the time, but it quickly went viral. Sonia even praised me during a conference call with the whole team.

Our current client was Dora Gols who was running against Raúl Navarrete for the governorship of a faraway state I'd never visited. When Gols hired SC she was up eleven points in the polls, but after a heinous debate performance—she was no Churchill when it came to her oratory abilities—and a slew of articles about how her family's construction business had made millions with shady government contracts, Navarrete was only five points behind.

As soon as I hung up with Sonia, I got to work on a short video that made Navarrete seem like he was dancing to Gloria Estefan's "Conga" in South Beach with hundred-dollar bills falling from the sky. (I must admit it made me chuckle.) Then I put together a few memes and tweets. Before sunset I was back in the reclining chair drinking a Tecate Light.

The following morning I took Goyo for a walk (his walks were getting shorter and shorter) and when I came back I found a man sitting on the doorstep. He wore dress shoes, jeans, a T-shirt and a jacket that was too heavy for the warm weather. His salt-and-pepper hair was in a flattop.

I asked, in a somewhat forceful tone, how I could help him.

He rushed to stand. "Good day, sir. My name is Ifigenio Baldosas Olguín, at your service." We shook hands. "I'm looking for the woman who lives here. Is she your mother?"

Was he a salesperson? I hated people who tried to sell me things. Again I asked how I could help him.

"My cousin Salomón, who works over in that house, told me the woman who lived here needed someone to wash her car, tend the yard and make some minor home repairs."

That definitely sounded like my mother. Ever since I can remember she's always on the lookout for hired help of some sort.

"She's on vacation," I said. "If you leave me your number I'll make sure she calls you when she gets back."

"Might you know when that will be?"

"No. Unfortunately." I took out my phone. "Give me your number."

"It's fine, sir. I'll be back. Thank you."

I felt bad watching him walk up the steep climb of the street that would take him to the nearest avenue where he'd probably take a bus. I would've hired him on the spot to take care of the house and Goyo, there was more than enough money in the freezer to pay him, but I couldn't leave the house in charge of a complete stranger, no matter how much I hated my mother at the time.

As always when I turned on my laptop in the morning, I drowned in a deluge of emails that Sonia had sent throughout the night asking me to do all sorts of things. The woman didn't sleep. Maybe that's why she had a twenty-something floor office overlooking Chapultepec, most certainly a luxury car and more money than she knew what to do with, and I was housesitting for my mother in my pajamas.

New accusations had surfaced about the Gols' construction business: they hadn't paid taxes in years, had built an enormous shopping mall in a residential area, and were suspected to have ties to a judge who always exonerated them of everything. The usual. After concocting some tweets, memes and replies for the bots, I went upstairs to my mother's room to watch TV with Goyo. I settled on a baseball game, like in the old days.

When I was a teenager and into my early twenties, one of the few things that soothed my anxiety was to get high and watch a baseball game. The one I found that day was Astros @ Yankees. Good enough. All I needed now was to find my mother's stash. (She'd started smoking in her forties to deal with her insomnia and early-onset rheumatoid arthritis. She hid it from Juan Carlos and I, of course. And I, of course, routinely searched for the stuff, as hers was of much better quality than what was sold at my school. She always knew but couldn't confront me about it because that would mean admitting that she herself smoked. It was our little game.)

I finally found the weed inside a handcrafted decorative mate gourd, but not before finding something else—a manila envelope labeled David that was hidden behind a painting. I took out the contents of the envelope and leafed through them as I rolled a couple of ultra-thin joints. They were the printed emails my mother had been exchanging for months with her high school sweetheart.

Forgetting about the baseball game, I smoked while reading page after page of the correspondence. (She'd do the same to me, I told myself to quiet the guilt.) The high school sweetheart was recently divorced and worked as a petroleum engineer in Cairo. My mother reintroduced herself as a recently retired bureaucrat and a widow. The truth was that she hadn't worked in over eight years since she was fired from the National Institute of Fine Arts for reasons that remain murky to me. As for the widow thing, by the time her second husband died, my mother had already been separated from him due to years of nonstop fighting.

All the lies in the letters made me feel for my mother. I couldn't stop crying, smoke coming out of my mouth and nose, as I read them. He spoke of his life in Egypt, complained of not having a good relationship with his kids, and tried to explain his job to her. She, being a news junkie, commented on Mexico's sorry political situation, reminisced about her youth, and never said more than half-truths about the personal stuff. In the last emails they planned her visit to Egypt.

All she knew was deceit, which led to loneliness, which she then tried to remedy with more deceit. Lies were the main reason we fought and why we weren't speaking at the time. Our quarrels always ended with me supposedly learning to accept that my mother was a compulsive sneak, but when she did it again, again I got angry. This pattern went all the way back to my childhood.

After reading the emails I put them back in their place and watched the rest of the game in a state of almost catatonic sadness.

The next morning when I returned from walking Goyo, Ifigenio was sitting at the doorstep, this time putting together a besom with twigs from the surrounding trees.

"Good day, sir."

"Ifigenio. What are you doing here?"

"Just wanted to know if your mother was back from her vacation."

"Oh, no. You must've misunderstood me." I felt bad. Who knew how many buses it took to get from wherever he lived—it couldn't be nearby—to my mother's house. "She'll be away for some time. A long time."

"You said you weren't sure when she'd be back."

"Not the exact date, no, but I know it'll be a while. She's all the way in Africa."

"Africa." It was as if he were saying the name of a newly discovered planet.

"Right. It takes twenty hours just to get there, so it's not like a weekend trip. You understand?"

"Africa."

"Sorry."

"Should I clean the yard?" he said holding up the nearly finished besom. "I can see through the gate all the jacarandas and bougainvilleas that need sweeping. And the cars need washing."

"Leave me your number and I'll be more than glad to pass it to my mother. I promise she'll call you. In fact, I'll make sure of it."

"I'll come back then. Thank you, sir."

He was there again the next day and we had a very similar conversation.

The day after that I couldn't take Goyo for his morning walk because Sonia woke me up before dawn in a panic attack. She wasn't happy with the team's work. (The only member of the team I knew was Sonia. During our group Skype calls, she was the only person on my screen, her shoulders always draped in a Hermès scarf. Every once in a while during those calls she'd mention someone's name with a question or complaint and a disembodied voice answered in one or two sentences.) We hadn't done nearly enough, she said, with the six-properties-two-in-Miami scandal. Hell, it hadn't even become that much of a scandal. In our new polls, Navarrete was within the margin of error of our client.

"*We're walking on very thin ice!*" said Sonia in English. Then back to Spanish: "Yesterday I fired Jorge just to calm the boss down." Of course I had no idea who Jorge was and wasn't sure who she meant by "the boss." "Today I want bloodshit. All day. Nonstop. CC me on all your submissions."

Bloodshit was how Sonia referred to intense trolling. It meant coming up with violently upsetting material for the IT bots to post on Navarrete's social media and blog. So say, for example, that someone clicked to expand a Navarrete tweet, the first reply should be a death threat. Or if Navarrete blogged about whatever, the comments section had to be flooded with pornographic images—preferably with Navarrete's face photoshopped onto one of the participants. When Navarrete put out a Facebook post, the bots were to be ready to spam it with offensive GIFs. The point was to make the candidate's digital outlets unnavigable for any decent human.

As always when I went full troll, by the time five o'clock came around my soul was hiding somewhere around my appendix area crouched in the fetal position, trembling. Goyo slept under the table, using my right foot as a pillow. He liked sleeping this way because then he was alerted if I left the room.

"Goyo?"

He turned to look at me.

"Wanna go for a walk, buddy? I need some fresh smog in my lungs."

The dog licked my ankle.

I don't know why I wasn't expecting this, but when I stepped outside Ifigenio was sitting there holding his besom.

"No," I said. "Please. Not today."

"Sir, I was wondering if your—"

"Not in the mood, Ifigenio. Tell me how I can get you to understand that my mother won't be back *for a long time*."

"Yes, sir."

"You understand then?"

"Yes, sir."

"Do you really? Say it. Say she won't be back for a long time."

"I'm sorry, sir."

I went back into the house with Goyo and slammed the door. My head filled with rushing blood and I immediately felt bad for the way I'd treated my personal Bartleby. After all, it wasn't his fault that my life had turned out this way.

Ifigenio was in his usual spot early the next morning when Goyo and I went for a walk.

"Good morning, sir."

I ignored him as I walked out with the dog at by side. While I didn't want to be rude, I also didn't want to continue this thing, whatever it was, that we were doing. Maybe if I weren't so nice he'd get the point.

He was there again when we came back—"Hello, sir"—and again I ignored him.

Sonia was in Guadalajara for a work emergency, so she didn't call me that morning. I did very little trolling. Then I went out to the reclining chair to smoke a joint while reading *The Economist*.

It was hard to relax knowing that Ifigenio was out on the doorstep. A grown man waiting for my mother to return from Egypt so he could work for a pittance. Ifigenio was a symptom of this rotten country, not the problem. The weed made me believe I could hear his breathing all the way to the backyard.

Still, I did my best to focus on the articles. I liked *The Economist* because I fantasized about working in the type of serious politics discussed within it: geopolitics, war, fiscal reform, trade agreements, etc. That was where I was supposed to be, not photoshopping pornographic images and making GIFs.

Goyo and I hurried inside when it began to rain. I went to the kitchen to make myself a sandwich and remembered Ifigenio. I opened the kitchen door and found him standing under the not-avocado tree with his jacket over his head. I waved him over and he ran inside.

"Thank you, sir," he said wiping his wet soles on the mat.

We each sat on an island barstool.

"I see you don't plan to stop coming."

"Have you heard from your mother?"

"I haven't."

"My cousin said she was very nice."

"If you're going to be coming here everyday, you might as well hang out in the kitchen. I'll leave the door open so you can come and go as you please. There's food in the fridge and pantry for when you're hungry. Stay away from the freezer."

"Of course."

"But I want to make it clear, for the last time, that my mother won't be back any time soon. You'd be better off looking for other work in the meantime."

"Thank you, sir."

The week leading up to an election was always the worst. During those seemingly endless days, Sonia expected everyone to work as hard as she did. Once, just before a close race in Tabasco, I was so tired and stressed that I flipped out when Sonia called me after midnight, cursed at her, hung up, turned off my phone and went back to sleep. At six the next morning an SC messenger showed up at my door with a wicker basket containing a six-pack of Red Bull, a box of caffeine-laced aspirin and a handful of Ritalin tablets in a re-sealable bag. The note, written on the back of Sonia's business card, said, *Buck up, cowboy!* Since then, whenever we got this close to an election I always gifted the contents of that basket to myself.

During the final week, besides creating the usual social media contents, I was expected to, for example, design fliers with false information about when and where the opposing candidate's rallies would take place and fake documents (contracts, checks, bank statements, and so on) incriminating him or her in all sorts of scandals. A lot of my time was spent writing fake news stories that our IT team then designed to resemble screenshots from actual news websites.

Goyo's lethargy became more evident as I, my blood bursting with stimulants, worked on my laptop, paced while on the phone with Sonia, listened to the television and radio news simultaneously while doing pushups, and tried to come up with new ideas. It always startled me when I walked into the kitchen to find Ifigenio sitting on a barstool, usually looking through a tabloid newspaper.

"Hello, sir," he'd say to me.

But I wasn't in a state of mind that would allow me to have small talk, so I'd just smile and walk back out.

I began to get paranoid. Who was this man? Was he desperate or insane? Maybe he was a spy. Surely he was at least a criminal.

I wrote a fake news story that went viral: Navarrete had been a member of the late-sixties ultra-violent paramilitary group Los Halcones. The screenshot of the article, supposedly published by *Milenio*, decorated with photographs of the Tlatelolco massacre, spread all over social media and for a couple of hours it even trended on Twitter.

Navarrete called into several television and radio news shows to deny the veracity of the story, something that should've gotten me a raise. He explained that of course he hadn't been a member of Los Halcones and that in1968, at the time of the student killings, he'd been a twelve-year-old boy.

"*You da man!*" said an elated Sonia over the phone. "I'd kiss you if you were here at the office."

"I can get there in fifteen minutes." This was only half a joke. I found Sonia very attractive and often fantasized about her and I doing it in her office.

"To be honest, when I first saw it I thought it was too stupid to work."

"You're the one who taught me that there's no such thing as too stupid in our line of work."

"The boss called me to congratulate the team and I told him it was all you." I doubted Sonia had given credit to anyone but herself. "Take the rest of the day off."

"It's almost midnight." She'd hung up by then.

I was too hopped up on Red Bull and Ritalin to sleep, so I went up to my mother's room, turned on SportsCenter and smoked a joint.

The Friday before the election, Ifigenio showed up in the kitchen with a plastic bag of tamales. It was the first piece of evidence I had that the man actually ate food. I'd presumed he took things from the fridge and pantry, but I'd never actually seen him eat.

He laid the tamales out on the island, two of each: chicken, rajas and mole.

"You shouldn't have, Ifigenio," I said taking a Red Bull from the fridge.

"You looked ill yesterday, sir. And you don't look so good today, either. Whenever I get sick it helps me to eat tamales."

"I look this way because I've been working too hard and haven't been getting enough sleep. But it'll all be over Sunday."

"You're quitting your job?" he said with incredulity.

"No, no. The elections are on Sunday."

"Elections?"

"Down south."

"I never vote. Don't even have voter ID. All politicians are a bunch of fucking thieves."

It was jarring to hear him swear.

"Can't argue with you on that, my friend," I said grabbing two tamales.

Gols and Navarrete were now tied in the polls, so that day I got twelve calls from Sonia, most of which made me worry for her sanity and my job. In addition to that, the Friday before the election meant that besides the impossible amount of work I was already doing, I also had to call people on the phone from 3-4:30 AM on their landlines asking them to vote for Navarrete.

Sonia had come up with this strategy during an election in Hidalgo. Call people in the middle of the night pretending to be from the opposing candidate's campaign, thus making them angry at our opponent. After the time we first did it, people were all over social media complaining about our opponent's disrespectful campaign workers waking them up. Everyone in our team had to do these calls and then send Sonia a PDF of our phone records to prove it.

By the time I went to bed, as I set my alarm clock for 2:46 AM with a joint in my mouth, I wondered how much longer I'd last in SC. It took too much out of me, physically and emotionally. It had made me forget who I was or at least who I wanted to be.

It seemed like a dream when, in the middle of the night, as I walked into the kitchen to make myself a pot of coffee in preparation for the phone calls, I found Ifigenio lying face down on the stone tile next to Goyo. No, it wasn't a dream. Were they dead? I sniffed for a gas leak.

I called out Ifigenio's name and his body shuddered as if lightly shocked by a faulty defibrillator. Goyo opened one eye, saw me, and closed it. He'd be dead in less than a month.

When Ifigenio saw I was there he quickly stood and tried to seem as collected as possible.

"Sir," he said. "Has your mother returned from Africa?"

"What's going on?"

"Yes, sir. Goodbye, sir. I'm sorry." He turned to leave.

"Wait. Let me just— How long have you been sleeping in the kitchen?"

"Sir, I—"

"Just tell me the truth."

"There's a man," he said. "An evil son of a bitch. Over by where I live. You know the type of man I'm talking about. He lent me some money. I had no choice, sir. It was for my daughter-in-law's medicine. She's very sick. And I haven't been able to pay this bad man. If I go back home empty-handed…"

"How much do you owe him?"

"Two-thousand pesos, sir."

"That's all?"

We were both embarrassed by my reaction.

"I'll just lend you the money," I said. "Pay me back when you can."

"I'll never borrow money again, sir."

"Don't worry. I'm not an evil son of a bitch."

"I made a pact with God."

"I'll just give you the money, then. No need to pay it back."

"I can't, sir. We'll just wait for your mother to return from Africa."

I must've smiled when the idea came to me. Not only would this help Ifigenio, but I'd finally be able to get some sleep.

"Come with me," I said leading him to the living room. I sat on the sofa and he took one of the chairs. Then I handed him a printout of the phone numbers. "You'll be working for me tonight."

I told him to go down the list of numbers, calling each one, making all the calls he could until 4:30.

"What do I tell them, sir?"

I handed him a copy of the script. "Just read this to them."

"Won't I wake them up, sir?"

"Yes. Don't worry about that. They'll probably hang up before you read the whole thing. Some will hurl insults at you. Don't take it personally. Move on to the next number. Got it?"

"Even if I wake them up I have to read this to them?"

"You got it. Fortunately for all of us, the job pays two-thousand-and-one pesos."

He furrowed his brow. "For one-and-a-half hours?"

"Why do you think people get into politics?"

"I see."

"Read the script to yourself a couple of times and I'll supervise your first call."

Ifigenio took his time reading the paragraph to himself with the utmost seriousness. Then he looked at the list and dialed the first number. "Hello, ma'am," he said. "I'm calling on behalf of Raúl Navarrete, candidate for governor."

I felt a wave of relief. In a few moments I'd be up in my cozy childhood bed, safe, sleeping.

Dog

Marissa Schwalm

[We loved this piece because, in the time of COVID (and even before), the American public has been obsessed with their dogs. This essay tackles the uncomfortable truths any pet owner has had to grapple with, and Schwalm does it with grace, humility, and earnestness. — ajt]

Four months ago, I realize that I want my dog to die. Not the old dog, fat and farting in the corner, but the young one—freshly six years old.

"He bit someone again," I say to Mark.

"Nips," he corrects.

A coworker this time, one who has a neurotic dog himself, who listened to every direction that I gave. *No eye contact. Don't bend down. No quick movements. Don't touch him until I tell you to. Stay in the kitchen by the counter when I let him past the gate. Don't ever—ever—put your face near his.*

"What do you want me to do? What can I do?" Mark asks. We are getting married in four months. We've been together almost a decade. What he really means is: *What can I say or do to make you stop being upset?* But what I really hear is: *We've had this same conversation so many times.* "You want me to put him down? Take him out the woods and kill him?"

My chest feels tight and I know that he could do it. Our house is littered with animal skulls on the walls that he's killed, and hides in the giant chest freezer in the basement. There's a skinning pole in our backyard. On his truck's dashboard are tails of small animals he's shot. He's a meat cutter by profession, a hunter and fisherman by birthright. He could do it. Take the dog out to the woods that we've gone to hundreds of times and shoot him in the back of the head with the .22.

I turn to him. "Yes. I want you to kill him."

*

Six years ago in Pittsburgh, PA, our third city together, there is an empty burning in my stomach. We live in a giant house with one of my best friends who I can't let go of. She and I barely talk, just pass each other on the way to the bathroom. Mark and I are moving to Boston in a few months and I know that I'll never see her again—she'll be lost to drugs and drug traffickers and I can't save her. So Mark and I drive out to the middle of the woods where a man has a litter of German Wirehaired Pointers. It's a shack of a house surrounded by woods where the scrappy-looking man walks us to a fenced in area where floppy and fat puppies fall all over each other. Mauser, Mark's aging dog, is a German shorthaired pointer and is classically loveable and we're imagining that the new dog will be similar; the breeds are basically cousins.

Mark, sucked into the tornado of my want, follows behind as I practically skip to the puppies. He doesn't want another thing to take care, doesn't understand my longing. *We already have a dog. And a cat. And are moving. Again.*

But spring is brand new so everything seems unusually green, bursts of leaves in the trees surrounding us. In the distance, chained to a post, is a large German wirehaired pointer and when the man sees me staring he stops chewing on his gums. "That's the bitch."

Some of the puppies, brown and white, sleep in piles. I pick one up and place it on its back to see how submissive it is. It flops over my forearm, stares up at the sky. Mark pokes at a few and looks up at me to say, *Well, what's it gonna be?*

*

Eventually, in each house we live in, a neighbor will wander out to find us. Perhaps we're getting the mail. Pulling in from work. Bringing in the groceries.

"Your dog," they say, wringing their hands, pacing in our driveway. "Every time you leave he goes nuts. It sounds like he's dying. Like he's going to come right through the window."

We shake our heads, grimace when they do, roll apologies out and out toward them.

*

Standing among the puppies my eye is caught by a brown spot moving up the hill toward us. The old man yells, "How'd you get out? Get over here!"

Squeezing its way through the gate he saunters between Mark and I, his little nub of a tail shaking. I pick him up and stare at Mark.

*

In Boston we live on a lake with dock that stretches far into the kidney-shaped water. The first time I see Kaiser jump off the dock after a ball into the water I'm taken by his sheer power. His body curves upward, his paws reaching forward. He swims outward until he grabs the ball and then turns back toward me, emitting a high pitch whine as if he is terrified of his own enjoyment. Soaking wet he finds his way back to my side and drops the ball, looking up, saying: *Again.*

*

The first time he bites me is when the UPS man knocks on the door; he's only eight months old. Barking a shrieking, violent sound, he tries to power through the door, the window. When I pull him back, he bites up my arm, chews, as if he's extending the barking onto my arm. I raise my shaking arm to my chest, feel my legs go weak. When I look up the UPS man, having witnessed it all through the doors, is gone.

*

On the car ride home, the puppy forms a perfect circle in my lap. The warmth of his tiny body travels outward from my legs, so that everything for a few moments feels okay. When we arrive, Mark takes Mauser for a walk before the first meeting. The puppy twists through our yard. He hasn't grown into the shaggy hair that the breed is known for, nor does he have the standard yellow eyes either. For now his coat lies flat on his back, his eyes are a radiant blue that I can still see as the sun sets in the backyard. Mark approaches with Mauser whose tail wags furiously. But the puppy jumps in front of me, plants his feet firmly into the grass, and emits a deep-throated growl.

*

We name him Kaiser. We joke that it's after the movie *The Usual Suspects*, though spelled like the German word for Emperor. In the movie, it's the name of the bad guy no one sees coming.

*

One day, when Kaiser has just about settled into our home, I see my phone light up with the name of my best friend—soon to be ex-best friend, a pain that radiates through me daily, the imminence of it. "Hello?" I ask, cautiously.

"You have to get home as soon as you can. The puppy…"

When I arrive I think of *Law and Order*, all of the crime scenes I've seen on TV. In Mark's and my bedroom the floor is covered in blood, small puddles of it seeping out from the corner where the crate sits. It smells of urine, feces, the sharp sting of iron. She holds the puppy, a towel wrapped around his leg. His eyes flutter, seconds from passing out. This will be the last time she and I ever ride in the car again, ever do anything together again after a decade of friendship. We rush him to the emergency vet who stitches up his leg that's been rubbed down to the bone where he squeezed out of the top of his crate in his raging desperation to get out, get out, get out, and find me.

*

The next time we move it is back to our hometown—Mark moves into his childhood home left empty by his brother, and I move an hour south for my Ph.D. program. At first I come to visit regularly but then a few months pass and the next time I arrive I stand at the doorway as Kaiser, who seemingly counted every minute I was gone, cries and whines as he runs back and forth around me. These aren't regular cries, but full on screams of loss, of grief, of joy at my return. Mark laughs at first but then grows silent—neither of us have ever seen a dog respond in this way. He whimpers and throws himself at my feet and as I bend down to rub his stomach I feel tears move out of my eyes and onto my cheeks.

*

At his full size he's much larger than we expected. In fact, he's huge. Mauser weighs in at seventy-five pounds and, before we know it, Kaiser towers over him. He's legs for days, a giant barrel chest, and scraggily hair covers every part of him. His eyes are shadowed by pointing fringes of hair, he sprouts a long goatee, and eventually he becomes eye level with a kitchen counter. He looks mangy, like a nightmare Jim Henson creature. Sometimes people ask if he's an Irish wolfhound, others yell out from a safe distance: "What *is* that?" But mostly when we walk down the sidewalk people cross the street.

*

The second vet, he lunges to bite in the face.

*

Out on our weekly walk of the canal in Boston, Kaiser seems to snap. A bird soars above him and he rears up, barking loudly, then he yanks the leash and pulls us toward it. It escalates quickly until he's twisting in the most unbelievable ways and joggers stop, people fishing turn, and I beeline it to the car. I gasp, my chest heaving, as the old dog lies down in the backseat and Kaiser barks his face against the window, leaving small circles where his nose presses against it.

*

Out in the woods on a snowy afternoon, everything covered in wet and heavy whiteness, I snap a dozen or so pictures of Kaiser and Mauser running, playing with each other, rolling in the snow. Mauser is stout, like a small tank, but Kaiser moves with a trot familiar to dog shows or dog food commercials. It's as if, for a moment, watching him makes an extension of me graceful, lovely. Flipping through the photographs at home, there's the two of them in one shot: Mauser almost posing for the picture, head turned to smile, and there's Kaiser—teeth bared, ears wildly pointing straight up, and his eyes that deep red and white color from the flash. I frame it, think that I'm somehow embracing the truth of the two them. Unlike my family, my fiancé, my friends or myself—Kaiser has no secrets, the worst parts of him are so present that it's often hard to remember the good things.

*

The first trainer, whose website is full of images of so-called aggressive breeds, comes to our house and never even sits down. He hands me fistfuls of pamphlets but he won't stop staring at the dog who snakes around him. Every time he turns toward Kaiser, the dog rears up. The trainer shakes his head and is in his car before we can even discuss prices.

*

I am not immune to the classic cute things that he does, the licking of the paws, the curling up into a tight ball on my feet, the nuzzle of his nose into the palm of my hand. I know the tender squeezing in my belly, just as I know what follows.

*

We try three different crates over two years, one even specially purchased that's supposed to be for airliners so that no dog can escape. He scratches until his paws bleed. I find teeth in the bottom of the crate. Most only last a week or two, and then, when we've exhausted the options, we hope that he can't chew through the front door.

*

I contact a vet through Cornell's special program for troubled dogs. "You're familiar with autism, right?" she asks as we go through his many symptoms—anxiety, panic, aggression, obsession, separation anxiety, destruction.

She suggests medication. She suggests looking into another trainer. She suggests as much physical activity as we can give him. As we're hanging up she pauses and I want to ask her about worst-case scenarios, the most horrible stories she's ever heard, so I can prepare myself for all possible versions that might be ahead, but instead she just solemnly wishes me good luck.

*

The second trainer we look into has us bring Kaiser to his training center, which is really a large garage off the back of his house.

He's a beefy man, all arm muscles and no neck. "Listen," he says, staring at Mark. "Dogs need a firm hand. They need to know who is in control." He points to me, "With a tiny woman like her there has to be a clear alpha so that he can fall into rank."

I sit up in my seat. Though I am small, barely 5'3, I resent his suggestion. I grew up with a German Shepherd, a Black lab/Doberman mix, and a pit bull. I used to walk massive dogs at the Humane Society for years.

"What you need to do is leave him here with me for two weeks.

It's a grand each week, but when you get him back he'll be perfectly trained." He reaches behind him for a black collar that has a little box on it. "We'll shock him into submission," he says, smiling.

I drag Kaiser out to the car and as we pull up the driveway my head shakes from side to side so hard that the horizon starts to blur.

*

While moving back home, I talk a longtime friend into letting Kaiser stay with him over a weekend. *Just don't leave any windows open, he'll go right through them*, I say. *Just be careful who comes over. Don't try to lock him in any room or anywhere—he'll get out.*

On the second day I get a picture on my cell phone. The friend's bathroom door is chewed through almost up to the doorknob—a ragged chew line right across the middle. *He shut himself in while I was out at the store,* my friend texts. In the picture, Kaiser is lying down in the background sleeping.

*

A year before we're married, I officially move all of my things up to Mark's once again and commute for my last year of my program. My mother mentions how often she sees my ex-best friend around town—in the grocery store, at a stoplight, walking through the mall—and I feel a mixture of emotions, but mostly the dull sting of loss. "You've always had trouble letting go," my mother says, and as she says it I don't picture the many boyfriends it took me too long to leave or break up with, or the friends who I held onto long after our lives had split in different directions, but the hairy, brown and white face of Kaiser.

He follows me around the house, sits or lies as near me as he possibly can. He pushes the door open to the bathroom and curls up on the bathmat while I shower. He was always my shadow dog, following me around instead of Mark, but now he seems to have crawled into my skin, made himself part of me. I wonder if a chorus plays in his head as he stalks me through the house: *never leave, never leave, never leave.* When Mark sends him to his own bed, instead of on the floor next to my side, Kaiser turns toward him and growls, teeth bared.

*

The truth is, I wanted something that was mine entirely. The truth is that I know his anxiety at a bone level, I know what it's like to shake and his reactions feel like every one I ever try to suppress come realized. The truth is, he never leaves.

*

There are many good days, normal days, boring days. He chews through his rawhides—the only thing he can have since no toy is strong enough, barks at the mailman, sits on the deck in the sun, convinces Mauser to play with him, and presses his face into my hand a thousand times a day.

*

While down at my Ph.D. program I had the cat with me and though Kaiser grew up with him we worry that the three years they are apart might be too long for them to entirely remember each other. I carry the cat inside, his small paws clawing into my chest, but keep him behind a kid fence so the dogs can smell him but can't get near him. Mauser wags his tail, sniffs in his direction, and then heads off to a corner to sleep. Kaiser tries to tear through the gate, emits ear-piercing yelps.

That night, as the dogs are locked in the bedroom with us, the cat wanders the house. I try to sleep but think of unspeakable worst-case scenarios. Mark snores in my ear. I want to shake him awake and say: *If he hurts my cat—now our cat—I swear to god.* But I'm not sure what I'm swearing to do. I'm not sure where the line is, what it would take.

The next morning, as Mark lets the dog outside, I sit in the guest bedroom that overlooks the backyard and convince the cat to come near me. He presses his face into my hand and sits down, purring loud protests.

Through the window, Mark tries to convince the dog to come back inside. Then there is a high-pitched noise, a squeal of some sort, and it seems to rattle and then grow silent.

I sit up in the bed, my throat tight.

"Marissa?" Mark calls up to me.

"What's wrong?"

"Don't come down here!" he yells.

I stand up but don't walk toward him.

"A stray cat. I'll—" he pauses. "I'll take care of it."

*

It is a fierceness to love something unpredictable, to love something wild. It is insanity.

*

Often at night Mark and I talk, especially after a bad day (Kaiser bites Mark's friend in the ass, Kaiser bites Mark's cousin in the arm, Kaiser growls and lunges at my stepfather when he wears a baseball hat in the house, Kaiser has chewed a couch cushion), about the future with Kaiser in it. Can we have children with this dog?

"I think he'll be okay," Mark says. "We'll do that baby blanket thing that people do, where they bring it home for him to smell."

I shrug. Remember the years I spent as a dog walker, the cruel irony of my inability now to control my own dog. One family on the day I arrived told me about how there was only one dog now, since earlier that week their Great Dane puppy was chasing after a ball and careened into a tree snapping its own neck.

I look down at Kaiser who, instead of on his bed across the room, is sleeping on the floor as near me as he can be.

*

In Mark's childhood home we've placed cinderblocks, handles of old yard tools, chicken wire, tent stakes, and anything else we can find up against the fencing. Though enormous, Kaiser squeezes through any gap, slinks beneath any hole, and digs so he can roam the neighborhood terrifying anyone outside. Our neighbor on the right stops talking to us and we even catch him one day spraying Kaiser through the fence with a bottle of Windex. More days than I'd like to recount I run up the street in my pajamas and slippers, a leash in hand, screaming his name, the neighbors staring from their windows. Oddly enough, off leash and outside his own house, he passes by people, is friendly to dogs, and trots along happily until I arrive and then he drags me, sometimes on my knees, back to our home as if to say: we are here together trapped forever.

*

Sometimes when I am out in the backyard throwing the ball for Kaiser, an activity that occurs often twice a day, I think about that Great Dane puppy. How hard would Kaiser have to hit the tree in order to snap his neck?

*

The third trainer is a smaller woman; she carries treats in a small pouch on her hip. She lets Kaiser hump her for many minutes upon their first meeting because she wants to see how long he'll do it. Mark and I sit at table, across from Kaiser thrusting his hips angrily against her. She teaches us some boundary techniques but warns us: he's a special needs dog, he will never do the things normal dogs do.

*

It takes me four years since the Boston bird fiasco to get the courage to take the dog out once again for walks. For an hour beforehand I try to wear the dog out in the backyard. We start out going only three houses up and then turning back. Two years later we've only progressed to the end of our block. The neighbors call out, "Who's walkin' who?"

When he's at the end of my leash I feel powerful, I feel like I know karate or could stop a robber. When we run up and down the same block, over and over, turning away from any conflict heading our way and our strides match, both of our legs hitting the ground in time, it all feels right. A surge of triumph lights through me.

*

Three weeks before our wedding we prepare to move once again. This time: Charlotte. Would Kaiser be less neurotic if we had only ever lived in once place, one state? I let the dogs out into the backyard and see the three little kids in the yard behind us chasing each other. It's the Saturday of Memorial Day Weekend and every yard around me is full of people barbequing, of sprinklers reaching out to the sky. I walk my lunch to the table on the deck.

As I step down I see the children pointing, their faces staring toward our yard. Mauser runs to the end of the backyard where Kaiser moves from side to side, jumping and barking. I move forward slowly, place my plate on the grill, and then hear the kids yelling, screaming for their mother, hear the piercing gargle of a cat. Then I'm leaping off the deck, tearing through the yard. In Kaiser's mouth, being shaken back and forth violently, is the black stray cat I had seen just the day before slinking through our driveway.

I look around, spot a branch a few feet forward. "Stop! Stop it!" I scream loudly, my voice echoing off all of the houses. It all sort of happens in slow motion, and then speeds up, then slows down. I see a flash: the cat's face, its yellow eyes. And then it is fast again, all fur and both dogs ripping and yanking and grabbing for it. I see another flash: Kaiser's teeth directly in the cat's neck, shaking, shaking. Then it is fast again: Mauser pulling on one end and Kaiser on the other. I drive the branch into both of them as hard as I can. I plead with cliché phrases: Jesus Christ. Oh God. Please no. Don't. No.

For a moment, Kaiser releases his grip and I picture it, the fantasy of this story: *And then, when I thought the worst might happen, the cat got away*. But it doesn't. He snatches it back up and shakes it one more time, hard.

*

Years earlier, when a man directly next door in Pittsburgh gets shot in the face in his driveway I am in bed alone, hear the shots, and look to the dog. He jumps to attention, sounding the alarm.

*

Through the years with Kaiser I find myself drawn to anything to do with special needs. I watch *Born Schizophrenic* and dozens of other similar TV shows, read books about Autism, non-typical family structures, and endless memoirs about families whose lives they imagined going one way but actually ending up drastically different. I see many parallels, revel in the similarities, but of course Kaiser is a dog, not a child. Mark wonders if I'm preparing myself for motherhood. I wonder what I'm searching for.

Each of these stories seem to have a moment where the parent or parents respond to the familiar question: "And if you could do it all over again, knowing everything, would you?" I always lean forward in my seat, watch the parents' faces, or read their words slowly and carefully, wait for one to say: "No, no I wouldn't. I would want something other than this." But they always say, "Yes, I would do it all again."

And when variants of that question, or even *Why don't you give him up? Bring him to a shelter?*, are directed my way I respond the most truthfully that I can: I don't know.

*

When young, my mother tells me about watching her neighbor shoot her new kitten dead for getting too near his pigeons. This is what I think of when I picture the cat's soft and slightly pinkish underbelly—that I have never seen anything really die. I lock myself in the bathroom, and every part of me shakes from the sobs. I want to be far away, walk out the door, and have there be only a white space. But instead, Kaiser pants on the other side, his nose rattles the handle, then he lies down, tiny tuffs of his fur sticking under the door.

*

One summer evening when the house is thick with air, Mark and I brush our teeth in the bathroom. I lean down, pull on the lever to the tub that the cat paws at so a small stream of cool water pours out. Kaiser, panting incessantly, strolls past me, steps into the tub, and joins the licking cat, their two tongues reaching out, both of their eyes closed in delight. Mark and I fall into each other's arms with laughter, and Kaiser steps out of the tub to rub his damp head along our legs.

*

The morning after the cat dies a most gruesome death, I pause before opening the back door to let Kaiser out. I stare at the backyard. I hope that the kids in the house behind ours stay inside until we move. I hope that wherever we go next has a better fence. I hope for things I can't even narrow down into words or images. Kaiser twists in circles, barks loudly, rears up until I turn to face him and then he sits—knowing the cue—and I pull the door open in one firm jerk.

Fractured Composition

Jennifer Harvey

[We loved this story for the way it highlights how memories splinter, leaving us with only the smallest pieces to hold onto. Harvey's writing is haunting and lyrical, reminding us with every line that "memories will come unbidden, and always when you are least expecting it." — AM]

1.

She once told you a lie. This was before you understood that lies could also be an expression of longing, a way of seeking out connections.

She told you a lie because she sensed, long before you did, that you held within you a need to believe such things were possible.

You told her: 'I had the strangest dream. There was this turquoise circle of light, that's all it was.'

You told her: 'I was floating, and the light was behind my eyes, all crystalline and blue. All peaceful.'

You didn't tell her how it shimmered and flickered. You didn't tell her that it left you feeling dazed and buoyed, as if you had been touched by grace. You didn't think she would understand that.

But she had surprised you. She had nodded and said: 'Oh, I know, I know', and then left you to believe you shared this vision with her. And you were happy to believe it. But that was before you discovered the many ways it would linger. As memory, as premonition, as foreboding. No, it was anything but a dream.

2.

And if it was a memory, was it this?

Years earlier, in some park somewhere, you are playing hide and seek. You tell her to count to ten while you run and hide, but she is small still, four or thereabouts, and so she messes up the order, goes from three to ten in one jump, then cries, '*coming ready or not!*'

You're not ready, and so you jump to the nearest sanctuary, some shrub or bush. And down, down you go, into the dark and dank and gunk of a drain. Popping close to the surface a moment later. Above, the light, frayed at the edges. You call and hear your own voice echo and bounce. Then a face there, above, looking down and saying something. Then, laughter. You can't remember who pulled you back to the surface. But someone must have. All you remember is the look in her eye. Curiosity mixed with fear and a gleam of something else.

It's not a shared experience, this one. Not yet. She has yet to go under. You have yet to watch her sink. For now, there is only that gleam. And the lifelong shiver the memory will contain.

3.

The premonition is darker, no light this time. It starts in the old house. In a room with a flimsy curtain that floats in the breeze. It lets the light in but shrouds the scene outside in a gauzy haze which makes you think it's always raining outside. You can't help but look at it and wonder what purpose it serves. Better to leave the window bare, have the sun—when it's there—pour into the room. It's cleansing, so they say, a fact you find rather pleasing as you lie there not wanting the day to begin. Because now something has been illuminated. You can feel it.

That curtain wafting in the breeze, like the remnant of something long forgotten. You remember seeing it before and knowing straight away where you were in a dream. The dream of the old house, the one you never want to go back to. Just the idea of it, had filled you with despair. And it was despair. It wasn't melancholy or nostalgia.

'Please, not there,' is what you had thought.

And how does it make you feel, to be back here again, back in the room, back in the house and watching the curtain waft? To know that dream was more of a vision, a casting of the die. It brought you here once more. Left you longing to slip back into sleep, into dreams. To get away. Far, far, away from here.

And the curtain flutters and lets the light in. Just long enough to illuminate something: '*You don't know what you're doing, where you're going. There is no away.*' And the truth of it makes you turn to face the wall.

But it doesn't help.

4.

It's the one thing they never tell you.

Memories will come unbidden, and always when you are least expecting it. You are galloping on a horse. You feel the pull in the muscles and lean forward, you and the horse, fused sinew to sinew. And then there it is, you remember her and understand the effort it will take to forget. How you will need to pull away from her again and again and again.

And you squeeze your heel into the belly and kick, but know the pull you feel, the rush as you try to push it all away, is but a momentary relief.

But still, you do it. You listen until all you hear is the thud of hooves on the soft ground, beating the rhythm of your retreat. Away, away, away.

5.

Before the turquoise light, before that shared dream, she tells you of a different dream she had once. No lie this time.

'I'm a block of ice and I'm melting,' she says.

And you think about that. You never stop thinking about it. It will always be the first thing you think of, when you think of her. That she called it a dream. Not a nightmare. That was the moment you knew something was wrong.

Though you never dared ask her, 'Who wants to melt away like that?'

She did apparently. And you need to find a place for it, for the impossible certainty you have, that if you'd said something back then, things would be different. You would be different, because you had asked her why she dreamed such things.

Instead all you have is her laughter. 'It's just a dream. Just a stupid dream.'

You could have told her, 'No, it's not. It's more than that.'

But instead, you turned your face to the wall again. Away, away. Gallop far away.

6.

A daytrip to a waterfall. You hear the rumble of it long before you get there and though neither of you say a word, you hold hands in the back of the car as your father drives closer. All you can think about is the edge, the place where it becomes inevitable, the tipping point where falling cannot be halted. Over and over and over you go.

Memory, premonition, foreboding.

You close your eyes and try not to think of it, squeeze her hand a little harder than you mean to, so she pulls it away and squeals, 'Ouch! That hurt!'

And when you open your eyes she's looking at you and she sees you are afraid. She sees the way the rumble of the water contains the depths of your fears. You have revealed yourself without meaning to. There exists an understanding between you now, that when her time comes, when she falls, you will not be there for her.

7.

Oh, and if you'd known it existed, this emerald valley, dotted with black grazing horses. If you'd known it existed for real, and not as some figment of the imagination, some dream, you'd have prepared for it better. Walked more slowly up on to the ridge and lifted your eyes with more reverence, more presence of mind.

As it is, all you manage is a sigh. A wordless appreciation. Just a lifting and falling of your rib cage. It feels like you're wafting, fluttering. Which reminds you of something, though you can't quite remember what it is. The past? The future? Her? Or is this simply the way time shifts? It is always meant to catch you unawares.

You stand on the ridge and look down and understand that it is this you should have dreamed for her. This valley, this safe-haven where the horses run to. Far from the rumbling water.

8.

The dark-eyed pick pockets were children really, but old enough for you to shout at them and slap at the hand you felt as it reached inside the bag on your shoulder. It was a stupid thing to do. Your own fault. They are trained to spot the opportunity and there you were, imagining you're Audrey Hepburn and dreaming of Rome. You're the seventh dreaming girl they've seen that morning.

It doesn't quite spoil the day. But it leaves you alert. Leaves you admitting you're not a carefree wanderer. Something you only fully understand as you stand by the Trevi fountain and grow dizzy as you listen to the water gurgle. That sound again. You came here hoping to drown it out with incense and incantations. Light a candle and illuminate things. Force out the darkness with light and prayer. But there it is again. The sound which will always follow you. No saints can diminish it. No horses can carry you away from it.

9.

When the day comes, it is déjà vu. Your parents are not the watchful types. They let you roam. Never know where you are. When she slips, they are on the riverbank, oblivious. Sitting with a small picnic and a plaid blanket, they hear a commotion. People on the bridge shouting, '*someone's fallen in*,' but they think nothing of it.

But down by the water, you stand and stare and wonder if this is the moment you are supposed to go in after her.

But you do not move. You simply stand and watch. You watch as she goes under. You watch as she sinks down, down, down. You watch her, and you know she is looking up at the circle of light on the surface, that she can see the bright blue beyond, but cannot reach it. And you smile because you share this now, both of you knowing how it feels to be pulled under, how it feels, to disappear from view. How it feels to look up at the light and despair as you hear the laughter.

And you tell her this as you stand on the riverbank and watch her go. You call out to her, '*I know, I know*.'

10.

And you dream again. Or is it more a reimagining, a hope? A way to forgive yourself? On this imagined day, you stand at the water's edge and see her resurface, see her pull herself ashore and walk along the path towards you. You smile and take her hand and lead her back to your parents who stare in disbelief as you tell them.

'*It was her. She's the one who fell in*.'

And you never let go of her hand. You keep it folded tight in your palm forever. You don't let her slip. You don't let her go. You hold on tight and say, '*I know, I know*,' as she tells you it was a lie. She never did have that dream. She never knew that presence, that sacred light which seemed to hover above you.

The one you always thought would keep you both safe from harm, but which protected only you.

Urban Theology

Gregory Lawless

[We loved this piece because it named a quintessential element of urban life with beauty and respect: the pigeon. It reads smoothly, makes us smile. "Urban Theology" invites us to look for holiness everywhere. — ajt & PL]

I run into the courtyard with a broom
to scare the angels. They're eating

bread crumbs and hotdog buns
from the ground and stealing

quarters from the fountain.
They flock from one tree

to the next as I wave my broom
around like a flag. They have dark

eyes and their wings are scarred.
They bite each other and me

with tiny mouths. In another ten million
years their teeth will fall out. But today

is today. Their haloes burn
away the leaves of the Norway

maples and singe the broom's
whiskers. Their droppings clog

the grates. Poor things, the angels,
bored to death by everything

they understand. Tell them a joke,
and they fall asleep,

weeping. They know every punch line
ever known to man.

–

Always and Forever

Ángel García

[I get chills thinking about this piece. It is (still) (unfortunately) timely. For people who have known the fear of being a brown or Black body in the United States, this piece will ring true. For us, it provided us kinship: the significance of being known. For people who do not know, this piece will enlighten. For you, it is required reading. — ajt]

On Being a Brown Body in a Red State

I thought of what I would do if he pulled the trigger. In the time it took him, seconds, to raise the orange plastic gun from his side and point it at my chest, I considered my options.

*

In nature, matters of survival are dictated by only two choices: fight or flight.

*

The first year of my PhD officially done with, I decided to clean. There were, undoubtedly, more celebratory options: 1) to go out and have a few drinks or, 2) to immediately leave this place and go home to Los Angeles. At thirty-five years old though, both come with costs. Drinking while brown in a red state is not a safe practice. I know this because of my problems with drinking—I can be an angry drunk—and because of who I might encounter at the bar. Over the years I've worked to control my drinking, control my anger. What I don't have control over are racist comments or conversations. If I engage, my patronage as a customer (no matter how much I spend or how much I tip) holds less value than someone else's unease with my presence. Traveling, the safer option of the two, takes its toll on the wallet. Leaving, as badly as I've wanted to throughout my first year, offers only a temporary reprieve. I can't afford to do either.

*

Instead, I washed dishes. Cleaned the stove top and wiped the counters. Swept and mopped the floor, vacuumed the apartment, and stepped out to discard the trash. Outside, when I turned around from the trash bins, there he was in front of me. A child with a gun in his hand: a neon orange revolver with a gray handle. The gun loaded.

*

I've had a gun pointed at me before. In this moment, there is a certain sense of familiarity: the first time I hold a gun I am five years old; the first time I have a gun pointed at me I am seventeen.

*

I've rarely felt safe since moving to Nebraska. If I do feel safe, when I do, it's a fleeting sensation. It comes and goes as easily as the weather; it's in constant flux.

*

At a red light, a convertible with four men pulls up beside us: we are four boys on our way home. The men begin yelling; one stands to flash signs. He reaches back down into the seat beside him and stands again. Before we see a gun, before it's pointed in our direction, my friend runs the red light and loses them up the street.

*

This is what happened: a seven-year-old white boy pointed a gun at me. A toy, but a gun nonetheless. Here, a white boy in a red state in a white country—where for more years than I have been alive men of color have been killed for less than this, nothing more, nothing other than walking out of their home, down the street, thinking about tomorrow, only to have tomorrow and every day after, taken away from them—deliberately and confidently, he raised a gun to my body.

*

In his essay, "The Artist's Struggle for Integrity" Baldwin writes "All safety is an illusion." Every time I've read this, with this point and this point only, I've struggled. So much of my experience in and around Los Angeles, by the very nature of living in or near communities of color, made me feel safe. I felt protected. At home or on the streets of LA, there was a constant presence: hip hop being played loudly on the radio of a passing car, Spanish or Tagalog being spoken while walking though the grocery aisles, people of color consistently and constantly interacting and living in community.

The comfort of diversity never negated my understanding of both the historical and contemporary manifestations of racism. I'm aware of the ways in which segregation, gerrymandering, exclusionary real estate practices, subpar educational systems, police practices, eminent domain, manifest destiny, urban renewal and gentrification have been wielded against people of color to regulate, manipulate, erase, exile, imprison and execute us. By the very nature of living in communities of color most vulnerable to structures of power—I, we, all of us—are under constant scrutiny and surveillance. Communities of color are always being watched: by camera or by clerk, by developer or police officer, by police and news choppers cutting through the night sky, their searchlights flushing people of color out of their communities like prey.

In Los Angeles, where there were more of us to "surveil," there was in response more surveillance. Despite this reality, I felt less surveilled. This, possibly, is wherein lies the illusion because the presence of people of color served as a reminder, in light of such experiences of social injustice, of survival. I was always reminded of the ways in which people of color, and by extension, communities of color have survived and continue to survive.

Here in Nebraska, it's quite the opposite experience. Because there are fewer of people of color to "surveil" there is less surveillance. This is complicated by the fact that white people are not surveilled in the same ways as people of color. Suspect, a word used as part of the police lexicon, is imbued with racist meaning and intention. It justifies profiling and detaining, it justifies interrogation and arrest. Ultimately, it justifies violence against people of color and their deaths.

In a red state, the feeling of being watched though is amplified. There is no reprieve or safe space. I am under constant scrutiny and surveillance. I am always under the gaze of others. What differs most here is that there is not the overwhelming sense and presence of people of color. What that means for me, as a brown man, as a Chicano, is that I am forever suspect, considered criminal, deemed dangerous. There is no going home here. There is no turning the corner and being embraced by those who understand and empathize. Consequently, I am always and forever in danger.

*

Soft words. Soft words. I could have kneeled in front of him. Could have told him that it was dangerous to point a gun at a stranger. Used soft words to make him understand.

*

Cars slow when they pass. Heads turn behind glass. When I've dropped off rent at my landlord's home, on more than one occasion a car has slowed or stopped to watch me. I look back. I stare. These are the few moments I make eye contact. I want them to know I see them staring. I want to implicate them in their suspicion. I want them to know that I know they stare because I am a brown man in a white neighborhood.

*

Luckily, my apartment faces east and west because north of my apartment, across the street, in a yellow craftsman home there flies a confederate flag from the front porch. Every morning, when I leave for campus, pulling out the stretch of my driveway, I see it as I leave home.

It flies, every day, across the street from me: a constant reminder. I try not to look because I take notice of the small ways my body reacts. As a man of color in a red state, there is not enough room for my anger. Instead I try to forget, ignore, avoid—the strategies of powerlessness. Most often, I fail. I look right at it. Stare right at the stars and stripes, notice the way it undulates in the constant breeze of a Nebraska spring because by ignoring the racism, I ignore myself. My own body.

*

At the stop sign, the car in front of me doesn't move. I honk. Slowly, it moves forward. I circle the block to find parking. The car pulls up beside me. We exchange words. The driver tells me I'm lucky. If he had had his gun he'd blast me. Before driving away, he threatens he'll catch me later.

*

It sits with me. I swallow and swallow each moment, like stones. They weigh. In Los Angeles, it was easier to respond. To lash out, to speak up, to yell and curse, to demonstrate my anger and then turn the corner and forget what had just happened. I could let go. But here, my anger lingers. I can feel my jaw clench and my teeth grind. I can feel my grip on the wheel grow a little tighter. My anger is like cud I chew again and again. It tastes of bile.

*

I imagine crossing the street late at night: I walk directly across the front lawn, past the home-made memorial to someone who has passed, climb the few stairs to their porch and pull the flag from its pole. Or, I burn it where it hangs. I watch it flame and slowly turn to white ash.

*

Even if the act of violence never occurs, the potential for or possibility of it happening is a constant reality. It is a survival mechanism.

*

I could have snatched the gun from his hand. Ripped it from his grip and maybe smacked him. Watched him as he waddled home, his face red. Crying.

*

I figure someone will come out the house asking in the dark of the night, who's out there? A weapon cradled in their arms. This is not about courage. That it is not about how brave or not brave I am as a person. Something tells me the consequences are not worth it. I could easily, and justifiably be a dead brown man bleeding on someone's well-manicured lawn and no one would be the wiser. The flag still flying above my already-cooling body.

*

I came to Nebraska to study. To study, I am required to teach. However, as a graduate teaching assistant of color, the costs of studying and teaching in Nebraska are inevitably greater. In the classroom, I am expected to teach about race and racism and examine the ways in which, using critical pedagogy, students can explore both the theories and praxis of antiracism. But on a mostly white campus, my body is put on the line. Not all, but many of my students are resistant and/or reject these ideas, as does much of the country. White people want to believe racism doesn't exist. Constantly, rather than teaching about antiracism, I must first "prove" to a class of mostly middle-class white students, who have little to no personal experience with race or of racism, that racism exists. But their denial of racism is also the erasure of my experience in the world. Unintentionally and unconsciously as I seek to deliver "proof" I am also erasing my body and my experience from the classroom because my experience as a person of color, as an instructor of color is not enough. It is never enough. I am not an authority. I am not a professional. I am not a middle class, heterosexual, white man whose very word is evidence enough to be deemed true. My experience, my voice, my body, my word is suspect to them. Unlike on the street where I must prove my innocence, in the classroom I must consistently prove my worth as an instructor and intellectual, beyond and outside of my body which serves as a constant disqualifier.

*

I walk back to campus, groceries in both my hands. I see four young boys running after another boy. One extends his arm. Guns shots echo up the boulevard. I watch them turn back, the gun now pointed in my direction. Shots pop off behind me as I run off through a side street. Their footsteps behind me, giving chase.

*

To greet is a must in my family. Saludar. Walking through the door, it's expected that we greet everyone in the room with a kiss and a hug—or a handshake, depending on the company. It's a sign of respect. As a young boy, the youngest of four, my world of make believe was relegated to battle, figurines made into forces of good versus evil and what determined the victor was not strategy, not size, but which side could inflict the most harm against the other. Weaponry determined who won. The person with the smallest arsenal lost. What was also true, always, was that GI Joe had no children. Han Solo wasn't interested in Princess Leia. Love and care and family were not part of the imagined narrative.

Often, when I would go to my brothers' homes, before greeting me, my nephews would point a weapon at me: a toy knife, a sword, a mini revolver with the quintessential red tip to distinguish it from a real gun. It became common practice to brandish or wield a weapon. And it bothered me.

This is nothing new. This is what boys do with the weapons they are given. What particularly worries me about my nephews brandishing weapons is that already, at such a young age, they had succumbed to violence as a way to solve problems. However, the larger problem is that for little boys of color, even play poses potential danger. In their front lawns or backyards, at the park or on the street, brandishing a weapon, plastic or otherwise, is one of the first ways in which boys of color will be criminalized and seen as harbingers of violence.

I sit my nephews down. Ask them to hug and kiss me. I tell them that I love them and that I expect them to put their weapons away. As important as this is—a small intervention—I know this won't save them.

*

I should have walked the boy to his house. I should have spoken to his parents. I should have told them what he had done.

*

Though I don't know and don't care to prove it, I suspect the boy lives across the street. I suspect it's his parents who proudly fly the confederate flag outside their home.

*

In elementary school, after being chastised, after being picked to read, after being given detention Anthony would quip, It's cause I'm Mexican, huh? All of us would laugh. It became a moment of humor in an otherwise often boring day doing lesson after lesson when all I wanted to do was go outside and play or read alone in a corner of the classroom.

As the year progressed, it became less and less funny. As much as I was familiar with the idea of racism, as much as one can be in the fifth grade, I "knew" that not everything was associated with race. Yes, certain things were. No, other things were not. I was certain then of my certainty. The police officers who would often stop us and harass us about our bikes or scooters and curse at us, a group of young children, were racist. Ms. Matsu, who struggled to get control of the classroom and who often cried in class because she was frustrated was not racist.

But what Anthony articulated, even in the fifth grade, would become a reality. A pelon, chubby, with cholo shorts and black hooded zip-up sweaters, Anthony was making sense of his reality, despite how I, a chubby Chicano who lived across the street from his family, differed in opinion. But this would later become a reality for me, a man of color. I find myself now, in conversation, after an occurrence, questioning whether what has just happened results from the color of my skin. It's an infuriating process because it lends to a perpetual denial of my own experience. The fact that I don't have the credibility and authority to determine the answer lends itself to a lack of surety. It drives me crazy. Being here alone, with few other students of color, it's difficult to articulate how these occurrences drain me and often, despite my best efforts, cannot be explained to my white colleagues.

*

Powerlessness feels like a perpetual shoulda, woulda, coulda. I make up all the narratives of what I should have said, would have done, could have done to remedy the situation I find myself in.

*

I rarely, if ever, when walking on campus or on the street, make eye contact with white folks. Women especially. This is how I maintain the façade of safety. If I ignore and don't acknowledge their presence, there is less likelihood I can be accused of something, anything. If I don't acknowledge their gaze I cannot be considered a predator, an instigator.

*

It's simple to dismiss acts of violence against men of color as them having been in the wrong place at the wrong time. But this is always the case. The potential for violence exists always in a singular moment. Often what people don't understand is that for people of color, men of color especially, these singular moments exist in perpetuity. They exist, as the oldie would suggest, forever and always. It's said that the average American is just one paycheck away from being homeless. The average man of color, similarly, is just one moment, one incident, one conversation away from either being the victim of violence or accused of inflicting violence. This reality, though it may never take place, always and forever dictates and dominates my behavior and my mental landscape. It is the way I exist in and maneuver through the world. My students here often remark during conversations about race and racism that things are better. Better for who? I ask myself. Better how? As much as I'd like to believe it, I don't.

*

Driving out of my driveway, I'm reminded of the harsh realities for people of color that still exist: in the real world as much as in my mind. I am not safe here or anywhere. And though this mental landscape is draining, literally causing me to be tired and frustrated, it is also how I survive. If I forget, if I slip up, if I allow myself to let my guard down, I could be killed. Even in the brightest moments of my life, this is something that doesn't go away. This is how I stay alive.

Dear Empire [#5]

Oliver de la Paz

["[This is your light]" is only one of a set of "Dear Empire" poems Oliver de la Paz published with us, but it stands strongly on its own. "Picture, then, the ghost of us," he shares. And so it becomes his mission to give life to the ghost, centering it in our gaze so that we have no choice but to look (and look closely). — PL & ajt]

Dear Empire,

This is your light. The generators are silent, private like a cloth over the photos on the mantel. The moon winks as it rains. This night is like the back of a throat. Belladonna black.

Picture, then, the ghost of us. On the ledges, frames back against the table tops. The power grid's gap stretches in longer and longer synapses. For miles, the once steady gleam of light. Now they shift in the wind.

Wax from the house candles drops on the sill, making a jaw shape as it stretches and descends. It sings to no one.

Two Poems

Craig Santos Perez

[In these poems, Craig Santos Perez walks us through the evolution of language and "the evolution of legend." Within these poems, meaning is always shifting and evading, just outside of our reach. This is how we make "an offering to ghosts." — PL]

[the tongues our legends lose]

At first, narratives were spoken,
on which all others stand. So we begin

again with an offering to ghosts,
with '*habitus*' and '*costume*.' We mark

the evolution of legend and the tongues
our legends lose. You ask, "*how will we save*

the stolen hours when only a particular dwelling,
that of the field, remains?"

We compare '*spine*' and '*building*,'

trace the intersecting angles from signs

to stairs we can't descend. We look
for the shadows already here to lengthen.

You say, "*it's more than 'in proximity,'*
more than 'near to know what here was.'"

We listen to a silence that only refers
to another luminosity, a compass

based on ocean currents, an anchor
to translate '*direction*.'

[to grow into scar]

'*Reservoir*'
might mean '*to grow into scar.*'
'*Arms*' never had the chance
to mean '*cradling*'

what was
braced inside you.
'*Arrival*' might only be '*a fossil
of skin.*' I pretend

it rains here to say '*home*',
which now means '*a small procession
of what's
no longer promised.*'

In this place, '*birds starve
the veiled sun*'
might mean '*a fire
failed to burn here.*'

What do we cross
but '*language given to shield*'?

Concealment in the Love Space

Adalena Kavanagh

["Concealment in the Love Space" flows through days and spaces with ease. A mix of engaging dialogue with straightforward but graceful narration, this short story creates and explores intimacy. A foreign place with familiar people, it still felt new to us. — ajt]

Pearl watched the door, but Dean didn't walk through it. The other teachers milled about the room, and snacked on the European cheeses and American junk food arranged on platters and in bowls. They all worked at the Happy Smile English Academy. The hosts were the lead teachers—a couple— and had lived in Taiwan the longest out of all of them, not counting the two native Taiwanese teachers who sat next to one another on the couch warily eyeing the cubes of cheese that sweated in the heat.

It was a potluck supper and Pearl was the only American who brought Chinese food. Her aunt had prepared soy sauce pork and tea eggs while Pearl's mother supervised, adding her own special dose of anxiety like a secret spice. Pearl's food sat, unopened, on a corner of the crowded coffee table. The hosts hadn't even cooked rice.

Philip, an Irishman, brought three foot-long sandwiches from Subway, the American chain. When he saw the cheese platters he stopped before the table. "Bless my heart, is that Gouda?"

Jane, a Canadian, speared a cube and handed it to him. "Someone better eat it. This cost a fortune at the Tiger Mall."

Philip closed his eyes as he swallowed, and then buried his hands in a bowl of potato chips. These were plain salted chips, not one of the fanciful flavors, like seaweed, or fried chicken, invented for the Taiwanese market.

Pearl watched the door. Dean was the reason she had come to the party. The other teachers made her uncomfortable. Between classes they complained about things like the foreignness of the food—which was nothing like the Chinese food they had eaten at home. They longed for delicacies like a real French baguette, or a good cup of coffee. Once they found out that she was half-Taiwanese, they became more self-conscious about their complaints. It didn't matter that she was from New York; she was just enough of a 'native' to make them aware of their pettiness. They faulted Taiwan for not being home, for having unfamiliar social cues that made it difficult to distinguish sincerity from politeness. Even though Pearl felt many of the same frustrations, when she was around the other English teachers, she felt defensive of the very cultural differences they criticized.

Dean was the only other teacher as young as she was. The other ex-pat teachers were a good ten years older than Pearl. They were making the best of a bad economy back home by teaching in Taiwan and saving money by living frugally.

Pearl and Dean met at the Happy Smile offices when he was covering a shift for another teacher he described as the Angry Lesbian from Detroit. (Pearl later learned that the Angry Lesbian from Detroit had earned her nickname when she turned down Dean's advances.) Pearl and Dean chatted between classes and he invited her to have lunch with him the next Sunday, which was their only day off, just like the Taiwanese.

Though she often couldn't understand him through his New

Zealander's accent they went on six very chaste dates on their days off from the Academy. He asked her joking questions about New York. Like, "Is the Bronx really up, while the Battery is down?" Then his expression would change and he'd ask more earnestly, "If I visited you back home, would you have me? Would you show me the places only true New York girls know?"

Still, he also said, "Taiwan's a country full of virgins." She hadn't been sure how to take that. Was she supposed to prove him wrong? They were on their second date when he'd said that to her, in his mean teasing way. To sass him back she pointed at a closed-up-looking building that had no windows. It was a love hotel, with a lobby that led to the type of two-way glass window used in police interrogation rooms. The customer walked up to the mirrored glass and spoke into an intercom. The entire transaction was anonymous. There was a sign in Chinese, and then in English the legend— "City is in concealment in the love space."

"That's where people go to screw if they can't do it at home." Pearl watched Dean from the corner of her eye. He reappraised her, and she blushed, not able to fake the attitude as her own.

Pearl herself had just finished school. Taiwan had always been a vexing place to her, somewhere she felt drawn to but repelled by at the same time. She thought that if she lived in Taiwan she'd finally learn Mandarin. She'd studied the language in college but usually read novels instead of practicing her vocabulary. She couldn't articulate what she hoped to gain by mastering her mother's tongue, but she imagined it was a key of sorts. Surely all daughters feel misunderstood by their mothers, perhaps not as literally as Pearl felt misunderstood by her own. Pearl's mother thought it was strange that she would even consider living in Taiwan on her own, instead of with her aunt.

"You don't speak Chinese. You can't read. You'll get lost."

Pearl slapped her hand on the table.

"Exactly! How else do you think I'll learn?"

Her mother cut her eyes away and sucked her teeth.

"You don't know how hard it is. You don't know how lost I am. How scared I am when I first come here."

Pearl straightened up in her seat to emphasize the nearly half-foot difference in their heights. "I'm not scared."

"You're too stupid to be scared."

So, Pearl lived with her aunt. She signed a yearlong contract with Happy Smile English Academy and immediately regretted it.

Pearl's mother came with her to Taiwan, intending to stay for a month, long enough for her to get set up, but it was going on two months and she was still there.

Pearl's mother and aunt almost made a sport out of imagining all the horrific things that could happen to her if allowed to navigate the city without a chaperone. They convinced themselves that Pearl would be abducted, raped, and killed if they didn't protect her. It didn't matter to either of them that she had lived in her own apartment with three other girls during her last year of college. Nor that Feng Yuan was far safer than New York, where Pearl regularly went to parties or rock concerts in dirty industrial neighborhoods and took the subway home alone, late at night. Her aunt was terrified to even let her take a city bus to work and harangued her son to ferry Pearl about. He was a student and kept hours that fit her schedule, but she could feel his resentment radiating from his back as they rode across the city on his motor scooter.

Besides Dean, the only friend Pearl had at Happy Smile English Academy was Lan, a Taiwanese woman. She wasn't a teacher, but a secretary. She was taking night classes so she might one day teach English. Until then, she used every opportunity to practice her English with Pearl. Lan liked to bring Pearl food. She brought dumplings and pork buns every day until Pearl complained that Lan was trying to make her fat.

Lan pinched Pearl's arm. "Are you trying to reduce your size?"

Pearl shook her head. "No, I just can't eat this rich food every day."

Lan smiled. "It's because your father is American. If you were Taiwanese you would be like this." Lan held up her slim pinky.

Sometimes Lan irritated Pearl. She liked to put things into neat categories and say, "We Taiwanese believe this…" or "Americans always think that…" Pearl wanted to shout, "How would you know if you've never been to America?" but she held her tongue.

They sat next to one another on the couch. Lan opened up the plastic container with the pork and eggs Pearl's aunt had spent three hours simmering. Without asking her if she wanted any, Lan picked up a piece of pork with chopsticks and held it toward Pearl's mouth. Before she could stop herself Pearl opened her mouth to be fed. When Lan tried to guide another piece to her mouth, Pearl stopped her. "I can feed myself."

Pearl stood up and walked out onto the balcony to watch for Dean. He was often very funny, and they spoke for hours the way young people do in order to make themselves understood, as if their pasts are deep veins to be mined for treasure and insight. She often felt Dean was the only person in the entire country she could really talk to.

Sometimes, though, he was just mean. He'd told her that when parents picked up their children and smiled shyly at him, he'd pretend to praise their children in a cheerful tone. He knew that they didn't speak English, so he said things like, "Your child is astonishingly thick!" in a way that made the parents think he was just tickled with their genius.

She asked him, "What if they understand you?"

He waved his hand in dismissal. "They never do."

She'd had notions of having flings while she was in Taiwan, but she was so cloistered living with her aunt, there was little chance of that. Even though Pearl studied Mandarin every day and was even starting to dream in Chinese, she felt awkward around Taiwanese men her own age. She knew they saw her, because even going to Circle K or 7-11caused people to stare at her, but she felt like an exhibit—for display—not for use.

In turn, she was fascinated by the betel nut girls who sat in glass cubicles dressed in lingerie, spandex, or sexy schoolgirl costumes and sold boxes of betel nuts or cigarettes. The way so many Taiwanese couldn't help but stare at her, she studied those girls whenever she passed a betel nut stand and wondered if their lives matched their outfits.

On one of their Sundays, Pearl waited for Dean and stood with her hip cocked, one foot in front of the other. A young Taiwanese woman stopped in front of her and said something, but Pearl couldn't understand her, so the woman reached down and pushed her knees together. Pearl could only stare at the woman with her mouth open in protest. The woman smiled at her and said in English, "Now you look like nice girl." The woman wore blue contact lenses that made her look Siberian. Pearl felt immediate scorn— another Taiwanese girl trying to look Western. Pearl's father had blue eyes, but of course Pearl's eyes were brown.

Pearl's own cousin told her that she was too strong headed after he'd heard her argue with her mother. He'd asked her, "Does all American girls talk like you, so loud?" Pearl just shook her head and walked out of the room.

One evening, when Pearl was grading student papers, her cousin invited her to eat shaved ice. Her aunt smiled and waved at them as they rode away on his motor scooter. They drove through the city and then they stopped in front of a storefront, except it wasn't a shaved ice stall. It was an Internet café. Her cousin motioned for her to step down off the scooter.

"What are we doing here?"

He pushed up the shield on his helmet so she could see his eyes. "Wait."

He walked into the Internet café, and handed a young man a few hundred NT. He motioned for her to enter. When she stepped inside, the young man pointed to a computer terminal.

Pearl gestured with her hands. "What's going on?"

Her cousin stammered. "Wait. Wait. I go see my niu pengyou. My sweetheart." He'd learned that outdated phrase in his English class.

At the mention of his girlfriend Pearl thought about Dean and wondered what he was doing at that moment. She sighed loudly to show her annoyance, but then waved her cousin off.

Lan opened the sliding glass door and joined Pearl on the balcony. She stood close to Pearl and they watched the street below. She pointed to a small ground floor entrance that was the same width as a double-car garage back in the United States, but had the kind of rolling metal gate only seen on storefronts. It was Lan's mother's house.

"In Taiwan people believe a woman should live at home until she marries."

Pearl nodded her head. She had a cousin who was thirty and still lived at home. "What if you never marry?"

"Then you never leave your mother."

"Why not? Why not just move?"

Lan sighed and shook her head with impatience. "Not possible. Maybe in Taipei, but not here."

Pearl thought she was being kind when she said, "You're smart and pretty. I'm sure you'll meet someone."

Lan laughed, and then frowned. "I meet many people. Still, it doesn't help."

"Maybe you're just picky?"

Lan cocked her head. "Picky? What does this mean?"

Pearl searched for an explanation. "It means you don't like many things so you can't make a choice. Nothing makes you happy."

Lan nodded slowly. "My mother thinks I am picky. She always talks about this friend's son, or that young man, but I always shake my head. She shouts at me. She says I will grow old and alone and deprive her of grandchildren."

"Why don't you like any of those men?"

"I cannot explain." Lan picked up Pearl's hand from the balcony. She held it between her hands as if to warm it. Then she brought it up to her mouth and kissed Pearl's palm. The air around them was moist, and even though neon business signs lighted up the street, the balcony was dark and shadowy. "This is why my mother thinks I am picky."

Even when Lan released Pearl's hand, she felt herself frozen in place. Though she couldn't return Lan's feelings, she could see herself going along to break up the monotony of her life, to see how it felt, to have something she could call experience. This made her distrust herself, knowing that boredom and loneliness weren't reasons to give someone else hope.

Lan took her hesitance as encouragement and she leaned in to kiss Pearl, but just as Lan's hair brushed her face, Pearl backed away and shook her head. "Don't."

Pearl turned and tugged at the sliding glass door. Embarrassed and sorry for Lan, confused because she was curious what might have happened.

When Pearl re-entered the apartment, she heard Philip inviting Jane to an art exhibit in Taipei. They would go during the weeklong Chinese New Year holiday. It was an exhibit of Chinese fashion through history. Jane mentioned that there was a large display of "lotus shoes"—

tiny slippers for bound feet.

"My great grandmother had bound feet."

Jane looked at Pearl as if she'd announced she was actually descended from an alien race. "That's horrible! Chinese women must have been the most oppressed women in the world."

Pearl rolled her eyes. "Right, because corsets were so enlightened."

Philip smirked but when he saw Jane's expression he frowned. "Hardly the same thing."

"Oh, what do you know? You're a man." Then Pearl walked out the door.

She ran down the steps and when she hit the street she walked down the block to the 7-11 on the corner. A spot at the window counter gave her a view of the street. If Dean walked past she meant to stop him and lead him to the love hotel around the corner. Pearl and her cousin had an agreement that he would get her at midnight. Her aunt thought he was at the party, mingling with the foreigners and practicing his English, but his girlfriend's parents were visiting a sick relative and wouldn't be back until very late. If Dean finally showed up, that would give them just enough time. He'd be grateful.

Pearl sat at the sticky counter eating a tea egg she'd fished out of the large rice pot filled with salty brown broth. Her aunt's tasted much better.

As she waited for Dean to walk past, she thought of their hike in the mountains the week before. He'd taken the bus to her aunt's house and they meant to walk several miles up to a temple that had been cracked and ruined by the earthquake earlier in the year. As they walked up the road a man puttered behind them on a motor scooter. He shouted at them, "Hello!" She and Dean stopped and said hello.

The man asked them if they were going up to the temple. Pearl was about to shake her head, no, when Dean said, "That's right, man."

The man beamed and patted the back of his scooter. "I take you."

"No, that's okay," said Pearl.

The man waved his hand. He wouldn't listen to her protests so she climbed on the back. She told Dean that he would come back for him. He let her go, not concerned at all. It wasn't until they had already reached the temple that Pearl thought of her safety. She pictured her mother back down at the foot of the mountain, thinking she was safe with Dean. The man smiled and waved after he dropped her off and went back for Dean.

When they returned, the man lifted his seat and pulled out a bag of snacks. "We eat, okay?"

After they finished eating, the man waved them in front of the temple and said, "I take picture, okay?"

Unhappy with the distance between them, the man pushed Dean and Pearl closer together. "One, two, three. Okay?"

It seemed wrong to stand smiling for photographs in front of a destroyed temple but the man gave them a thumbs-up and placed his camera away carefully to preserve the evidence of his new foreign friends.

The man chatted with Dean and Pearl became irritated, their afternoon alone ruined by this encounter. Also, the man didn't seem to know that Dean was teasing him.

"Do you think I am handsome boy?" The man's fat cheeks pressed against his glasses as he smiled, waiting for an answer.

"You're fucking gorgeous, man." Dean winked at Pearl.

Pearl kicked Dean. "I think you're handsome."

"Good. I think I go to Hong Kong and be big movie star."

Pearl raised her eyebrows in surprise.

"I just joke. I study eco-no-mics. I make hen duo qian." He held his arms wide apart to show how much money he expected to make.

When they were back in front of her aunt's house Dean leaned in to kiss her. This was what Pearl had wanted— an hour or two alone with Dean, his breath on her neck, her hand on his back. Then her mother opened the sliding door and said, "Good. You're back. Dinner's ready." When her mother walked back into the house Dean pulled her close, but when Pearl invited him inside, he pulled away and said, "I couldn't stand another bite of Chinese food today." He kissed her, but soon broke off. "Anyway, what's the point? We can't do anything. It'll just drive me mad."

She blushed, pleased. She tugged at his arm and tried to pull him toward the door, but he stood his ground. "I wasn't joking Pearl. I'll die if I don't find some relief."

Pearl pouted. Dean traced a finger down her face and her mind went frantic as desire surged through her. She tried to think of a place, any place, for just five minutes. His frustration was hers, but before she could find a solution Dean moved away.

"Right. See you tomorrow."

Pearl watched him walk down the road toward the bus stop and took a step to follow him, but the houses were so close together, the only privacy was further up the mountain amid bamboo groves and the threat of mosquitoes— not suitable at all.

She joined her family but ate quickly so she could lie on her bed and relive his finger tracing regret on her skin.

Before she and Dean met, he'd spent all his money traveling in South East Asia. Pearl pictured him sleeping with carefree expat girls in humid hostels and was jealous. Since he was trying to save money he lived in an all-male dormitory where guests weren't allowed. It was true. They were never alone.

Then Dean walked past the 7-11. Pearl knocked back her stool and ran outside. She grabbed him from behind and reached up to cover his eyes with her hands. "Guess who?"

He stood still, as if this happened to him all the time. "It can only be my dear precious Pearl. You've got at least three stone on most of the girls around here."

That wasn't what she'd wanted to hear, always conscious of her weight compared to Taiwanese women. Still, she told herself that he was joking, and when he turned to look at her they kissed.

Pearl's cousin rode past on his scooter. He was early. Pearl wanted to turn and run down the street. If Dean chose to follow her, all the better, but she was tired of being tied to someone else's schedule.

Pearl saw her cousin park his scooter in front of her co-teacher's building about twenty feet away. Lan was standing there. Pearl wished she would go away. She felt responsible for Lan's desire and would rather pretend that nothing had happened. It was different here. Girls walked arm-in-arm down the street, or held hands, and it didn't mean anything. What happened with Lan didn't have to mean anything.

Pearl's cousin turned around after Lan pointed toward her and Dean.

She knew she wasn't going to take Dean to the love hotel. Even if her cousin had stuck to their plan, she would have only hinted at it, hoping Dean suggested the love hotel himself. That didn't mean they couldn't go to the party like a normal couple, instead.

Her cousin motioned for her to hurry. Instead, Pearl shouted, "You're early. You can wait for me this time."

Her cousin didn't understand her so he turned to Lan to ask her to translate for him. Pearl couldn't hear them, but she saw the sneer on Lan's face, and her cousin's exasperation.

He walked over to her. "We go home."

Pearl shook her head. "No. You can wait for me like I waited for you." She looked at Dean, who had an amused expression on his face.

"We want to stay."

Lan walked over. "Your cousin wants to study. You should go home." Lan looked Dean up and down, clearly unimpressed with him. This made Dean laugh.

Pearl blew out a breath. "Not that it's any of your business, but he didn't care about studying when he was with his girlfriend. We're going to stay."

Lan flinched. "American girls are very selfish."

Pearl's cousin was confused. He stepped forward as if to keep them apart.

Dean shook his head and caught Pearl's eye. He gestured with his chin toward Lan. "What did I tell you? A country full of virgins."

Pearl looked at Dean. His eyes were small and watery gray; they often danced with amusement, but she'd had enough of his laughing contempt.

"You always say the wrong fucking thing, Dean."

"It's the truth, isn't it?" When Pearl looked away he said, "You don't have to listen to them. You don't have to be a good girl for once in your life."

Pearl bit her lower lip. She wanted to stay and sit next to Dean and speak English without having to think so hard the way she did when she tried to speak Mandarin with her cousin or strangers. But how would she get home?

Dean looked down his long nose at her. "Suit yourself. I've had enough of this."

Pearl threw her hands up in the air and said to her cousin, "Let's go. I'm sick of everybody."

Pearl followed him to his motor scooter and strapped the heavy helmet to her head. She turned to see if Dean was still behind them, holding out hope that he would beg her to stay. Dean wasn't there. He'd gone to join the party without her.

Lan stood in the street, hunched over. She hugged herself as if she was cold, or had a stomachache. Her eyes tracked Pearl's every move. Pearl shook her head.

She turned to climb up behind her cousin. When they motored away the air felt good and cool on her hot cheeks. Her chest was tight, ready to burst with everything she wanted to shout but couldn't. Who would understand her, anyway?

Altar Call

Darise Jean Baptiste

[DJB's "Altar Call" opens, "Philonia received the scariest phone call she never imagined, she prayed that her affair with a married man would remain a secret to her mother." The line packs a punch—but is a guise. This is not a mistress story trope. It's Philonia's coming-to-age story; she claims agency and tackles generational demons. — TS]

The morning after Philonia received the scariest phone call she never imagined, she prayed that her affair with a married man would remain a secret to her mother. "Please don't let Mom find out, God, please." She recited that prayer like a chant, fast and throaty, until her dry tongue and chapped lips became unbearable.

The woman on the other end said she was going to wreck Philonia if she didn't stop messing with her man. Philonia didn't believe the woman would ever have the opportunity to hurt her. Grown people don't just pick fights, she thought. But she knew by the fury in the woman's voice that she was capable. Suddenly she felt too weak to hold the phone to her ear.

"He's sleeping right beside me," said the woman, who sounded outraged that she could or would ever have to have that conversation while he slept. Then her tone changed and she became boastful: "He will never leave me."

"Who is this?" Philonia said, feigning confusion. She had never seen the woman or heard her voice before then, but there was only one possibility.

"Bitch, don't play with me. I will rock you!"

"You have the wrong number." Philonia rushed the words. "Don't call me again."

Philonia tried to hang up the phone, but her hands shook so badly that she couldn't connect her finger to the END CALL button on the first attempt. She tried once more, then dropped the phone on the bed beside her. Grateful for the gift of being alone, she put her hand on her chest and wiped the dew that gathered above her lip. Then she slid along the spine of her mattress, resting her head on the edge of her pillow and nosing the excess pillowcase. She switched the phone to vibrate and within seconds, it began to bump against her hand. When it finally stopped and she could recount the night's events without interruption, she decided that she had been assaulted by a crazy gal making outrageous threats. She was convinced that she didn't deserve to be threatened even if the woman had the right phone number and she was in fact, sleeping with her man. She lay there for almost an hour, shivering in her own sweat, trying to picture the moment that her boyfriend exposed her identity to his wife. When the thought of betrayal ballooned in her mind, she buried her head deeper into the pillow, pressing down on the invisible pricks of "should've known better."

When the phone vibrated again, Philonia answered without saying hello. "How did you get my phone number?" She spoke unlike herself, demanding and impatient.

"Philonia, you all right?" Ava's sugar-crusted bark roused her daughter to full consciousness.

"Oh no! What time is it?"

"Half past seven. You're late for work and I could have used your help opening the bakery," Ava said.

"I'm sorry, Mom, I'm on my way."

"What did you mean when you said, 'how'd I find your phone number?'" Ava asked.

"Never mind," Philonia said. "I'm sorry."

Philonia listened to Ava complain of a pinch in her wrist that morning after the woman called. She offered to massage peppermint oil into her mother's joints once the devil's pies had finished their time in the oven, but then a line of customers had formed, and then lunchtime arrived, and then her father had called to check in on things. Skillman stayed home, on doctor's orders, since his heart attack. There he monitored the bills and thought of ways to increase business profit, always calling the bakery and asking to be put on speaker after The Young and the Restless finished airing. "We could up the price of the devil's pies by twenty percent," he said. "Folks will do anything for that creamy cocoa filling."

"He's right, Mom," Philonia said, careful not to show him too much favor. "There's nothing like your pies anywhere."

"Uh-huh," Ava yawned. It wasn't long before she sensed him tiring of her cold reception. "Oh look, there's a customer who needs help," she said, and abruptly ended the call.

"You don't have to be like that," Philonia said.

"Yes I do."

"The bakery only breaks even. Doesn't that bother you?"

Ava shrugged and returned to the pleasure that she found in baking. When the brushed butter on the pie crust shimmered like sunlight kissing the citrine crystals that she kept on top of the cash register, her smile lingered long enough for it to seem indecent to ask why. The bitter burst of cocoa nib in her mouth tickled her and she patted the little corner of her face where her jaw met her neck and quietly squealed. Skillman hadn't spoiled those things for his wife.

"You really should consider Dad's idea," Philonia said.

"Making more money isn't an issue for me, it's your father and his dirty habit."

"What?"

"He's been trimming the top of our account for months and giving it to his woman," she said. "I'm no fool."

That couldn't be right, Philonia thought. He'd never do such a thing so cruel, especially not after reckoning with the hospital bills from his heart surgery. She wanted to defend him the way that she'd want someone to try and make sense of her own scandal.

"He's not seeing her anymore," Philonia said. "Besides, he would never do that to us."

"How do you know? The next time you see her at BJs, you should ask her when is the last time she's seen him."

"Why don't you ask her yourself?" It had been a couple of months since Ava found out about her husband's mistress. She had bawled in Philonia's arms, enacted a brutally long silent treatment against her husband, and declared a ban against the woman's employer. She petitioned Philonia to buy the bakery's supplies elsewhere, but the savings at BJs were too good to deny. So, since Skillman's heart attack, she asked Philonia to do all of the shopping.

Philonia and Skillman met Yvonne one autumn day when holiday orders flooded the bakery. She summoned them to her line and quickly started to ring up the cases of flour they needed. She wore metallic blue eyeshadow and bell-bottomed pants. The sleeves of her brown and gold chevron print leotard peeked beneath her uniform polo. Skillman asked her for her name.

"She was friendly."

"She's fast and knows we need to get back to the store," he'd said while unpacking the shopping cart into the car.

"You told her about the bakery?"

"We talked it up a bit when you went to grab another case of flour."

She didn't think much of them talking until a week after Skillman's heart trouble when she journeyed to BJs alone and upon seeing Yvonne's made down face, got orders to tell her father to contact her, for she had something to make him feel better. Philonia wrinkled her face, which prompted Yvonne to explain that she had a drink that would help his heart regain strength. She pulled a small bottle of cloudy liquid from her pants pocket. "Tell him to drink it straight and hot," she had said. Yvonne sounded loopy, like she had tested the potion that might make his heart slower than it should. The idea of a steaming cup of unidentifiable liquid made Philonia think of her mother, who wouldn't eat for two whole days and only drank tea and whiskey when her father had to be rushed to the hospital. Her mother had only wished to make her husband feel better too.

"How did you know he was sick?" The dinging sound of barcode against scanner got loud and so fast that it began to mimic a broken record. Philonia wasn't sure if Yvonne had heard her question, so she asked again.

"I'm the one who told the ambulance to take him to Einstein and not Misericordia." Yvonne held her hand to her heart. "I heard the patients rarely die in white hospitals and when they do, the family gets to say goodbye."

In the parking lot, Philonia held the bottle to the sunlight before throwing it on the ground where its contents lay flat and helpless.

"You need to leave right now," Philonia pushed herself away from the woman's clutch. The woman twisted Philonia's shirt so tight in her fist that Philonia heard the woman's knuckles crack. When she got free, she put her hands on her hips and tried to stop shaking.

"I'm not going to tell you again. Next time I'm going to show you that I'm serious," said the woman. She flew out of the bakery, taking all of the sweet calm of resting pies with her.

"Stay away from here!" Philonia said to the swinging door. As she turned to face her mother, she saw Ava run to the back of the store.

Ava wouldn't look at Philonia. Instead, she hid between two aisles of baking supplies and carry out containers. Philonia called her name and begged her to talk. "I'm sorry you had to see that," she said while straightening her shirt collar.

"You're screwing a married man? That's lower than low." Ava paced the aisles and pulled at her hairline.

"Mom, calm down. I've got it under control."

"I can't believe you," Ava said. She let out a scream into her palms. "Women like you have made my life a living hell."

"Women like me?"

"Naive, irresponsible, impulsive," Ava scoffed. "I bet you think that woman won't run up on you again because you told her not to."

Philonia looked at her trembling hands and realized the possibility of another, more physical confrontation. She didn't want to talk about it anymore. She was scared and embarrassed and the secret that she didn't want her mother to know, was now as naked as the nights she spent with her boyfriend.

"Like I said, I'm sorry. Now will you help me reopen the store?" Philonia said as her mother took up the pacing again. "I don't see why you're so upset. If you hate what dad did so much, divorce him."

Ava flared her nose and raised her hands over her head as if some goddess would descend from the pantry ceiling to rescue her from her daughter's simple advice. "I took vows and I'm not throwing that away. It's the hussy who needs to take a hike, not the wife." She pushed Philonia out of the way, knocking over a bag of flour. "That woman was right for coming here and warning you she'd beat your ass."

They reopened the store and sold out of devil's pies before closing time. Ava and Philonia worked silently, waving off disappointed customers looking for an after-dinner fix. After they cleaned up and counted the money, Ava apologized for what she'd said.

"You deserve better than someone's seconds. I don't think you've really given love a chance. I mean, you're only 20 and stunning, home from college for the summer. Why settle for someone who's already been around the block?"

"I make him happy," Philonia said, while opening a cabinet door, which hid her face. "That makes me happy." She wondered if Yvonne's reasons were the same. Yvonne didn't seem to be a terrible person. She might have saved her father's life.

"You need other people in your life who can make you happy," Ava said. "Come with me to my women's group. It'd be good for you to meet folks who thought they couldn't quit a man even though their hearts were being pummeled. I'm going tomorrow. You should come."

Philonia hesitated, waiting for Ava to leave the pantry first. She took out the trash bags that sat near the dumpster door. There were two — one bag looked easy to carry but had a gray pool of dank liquid forming under it; the other bag was bloated and looked like it would hurt her back. She couldn't decide which one to hoist into the dumpster first.

Philonia woke in the middle of the night to the trenchant sound of ringing, ringing, ringing. She thought that it would stop after the fifth round, but it went on until she counted nine. Finally, her phone sighed, then its rectangular face beamed neon, signaling a voicemail.

She felt the same phantom stomach punch that she felt when her boyfriend's wife confronted her at work earlier that day. She replayed the woman's razor-sharp words in her mind. "Bottom bitch," the woman had said, while pointing at Philonia. Her triangular-tipped nails mocked knives and compelled Philonia to flinch.

Her phone went dark and quiet. She relished the notion that she wielded power in her passiveness. She listened and concentrated on the wife's raucous voice and braced against the sounds of lurid phrases — "trashy ass ho" and "pathetic hoochie" — like punches from an angry mob. The cuss words, one by one, landed on her head. She lay there, wondering how long before the woman would lose it entirely and throw a fist. No, they were mostly empty insults, she reasoned. Yet she couldn't shrug off the threats to her body. "I won't stop calling until you're out of our lives," the woman said in her message. Philonia decided that she had to quit her boyfriend, but she wanted to tell him first.

"Are you ready?"

"Meet me out front."

They got into the car wearing their Sunday best. Philonia hadn't been to church since middle school, but she remembered the fullness of that communal gathering. The day the woman confronted her at the bakery, Ava reminded her of how isolating shame could be.

"Do you blame me for what Dad did to you?"

"Why would I blame you?"

"I didn't have to tell you about Yvonne."

"I don't blame you, I just don't want you to ever think that I'm on your side in this mess you're in. A part of me wants to smack you the way that woman said she would." Ava turned off the car and stepped out. Philonia followed her into a storefront next to a church on East 225th Street.

A woman dressed in black and wearing a button that said "Love God Herself" answered the door. Ava introduced Philonia and asked if anyone else had arrived yet.

"Everyone's here."

The space was a dimly lit, railroad style room with tealights lining the floor. Soft piano music played while two other women stood near a coffeemaker that was set up near a barred window. A sign-in sheet on the folding table read, "Meeting #57" on the top. The other women waved Philonia over and began introducing themselves. She could tell that she wasn't the youngest by the way one attendee meticulously styled her baby hairs, a style she too wore. Another woman had a baby bump. The woman in black joined them, flashing a gummy smile.

"You look just like your mother," she said.

"I don't mean to be rude, but, is this a cult?" Philonia asked.

The women's laughter settled her. She exhaled, glancing her mother on the other side of the store.

"This isn't a cult," said the one in black. She laughed some more as she poured herself a cup of coffee. "It's like mediation meets meditation circle."

"Meets survivor group," chimed the youngest one.

Philonia twisted her face and looked to Ava for confirmation. She felt set up by her mother who was preoccupied with her wallet.

"Lover's betrayal is no joke," said the woman in black. "Being here helps me deal with the fact that my ex-girlfriend cheated on me with her boss and now they're buying a house."

The sound of coins and keys clanging as Ava ruffled through her purse stole Philonia's attention. Finally, Ava joined the group of women and handed an envelope to the pregnant one. "Count it before you leave."

Philonia watched the woman hug Ava, but quickly looked away when Ava raised her forlorn face from the woman's shoulder. She thought of her father skimming funds from the bakery and handing Yvonne envelopes full of cash whenever he'd meet her. Then she thought of the time her boyfriend had given her a few hundred dollars to treat herself to whatever she wanted. She got her hair braided and saved the rest.

"Shall we get started?

"Does anyone have an offering for the altar? Set down the thing closest to your current suffering."

Like monks entering a monastery, the women filed toward the wooden table at the center of the store, where anything could have taken its place — a cash register, a stove, a condiment stand. Once each woman returned to her seat, Philonia saw that there was still space on the altar. She pitied its nakedness, its scratch marks deserving of adornment. So she dug into her shirt and pulled out the heart charm that her father gave her when she graduated high school. She slowly removed the jewelry from around her neck and placed it on the dented surface.

"The item that lies on the altar," Ava started, "is merely a symbol of the burden that brought you here today and its destruction represents the erasure of that turmoil." She exhaled. "In the same way that ash can be lifted from the earth, so will your burden."

Philonia waded in an ocean of confusion. Her mother was onto something with her words, but she couldn't fully grasp it in her hands. She felt guilty about that.

"What happens to the things on the altar?" she wondered aloud.

"Don't worry, you can take back your things if you want to," the pregnant woman said.

Philonia felt relief; she adored the charm, silver and heart-shaped with the letter P engraved in the center.

"Your burden is removable, just like the shoes on your feet," Ava continued.

Her cadence had a hypnotic effect on Philonia. She told the women to be strong as she lifted the ends of her words and passed them over like plates to her daughter and the other women. Philonia had trouble believing she could follow Ava's command, so instead she let the music of her mother's words melt into her like a salve.

Ava lit sage and waved it above the altar, the smoke snaking around her neck, forcing her eyes shut. The woman in black stood up from her seat and took the sage from Ava. She waved it over her own body and then passed it to the next woman, who passed it to the next woman, who passed it to Philonia.

"Do I do what you just did?"

"Follow your intuition," Ava said. "Find it and follow."

Philonia held the sage like a paintbrush, sending it up and down the length of her torso. She felt awkward and amateur.

"Here, I'll take it." The pregnant woman blew out the small fire and turned to the group. She spoke about preparing to raise a child alone after she thought her lover would leave his wife to be with her and his baby. Her baby's father ghosted her soon after his wife found out that she was pregnant. The wife made him vow to never see his new family or she'd ruin his whole life and tell their kids. She thanked the group for helping her choose a name for the baby.

"Don't you ever wonder about the wife?" Ava asked. "How do you think she'll cope with what her kids don't know?"

"At times I do," the pregnant woman said, rubbing her baby bump. "But more often I find myself trying to figure out how to forgive myself before little Judge arrives."

Would knowing the gritty details of her father's infidelity have prevented Philonia from sleeping with a married man? Probably not. Their affair was not meant to last long enough for her to apply someone's lessons learned to her own recklessness. She'd never spent more than 24 hours at a time with him; she liked the way he ignored large portions of his life just to experience a short escapade with her.

Philonia never heard her mother say the name of the woman who slept with her father. Though Philonia was unaware, she had adopted this no-naming practice from her mother. She almost never spoke the name of the man she was seeing. He was saved in her phone as Him. He, on the other hand, took joy in calling her name. Philly.

"She won't bother you again," he said. "Philly, don't do this."

"I can't see you anymore."

"Just once, to say goodbye. Philly, I need to see you once more."

"You should have protected me. No one was supposed to find out."

"Philly," he whispered. "I never meant to hurt you."

She listened to him breathe and she took his silence to mean patience. He'd wait for her. The phone's heat on her ear spread over her face and down her neck, past her chest and stomach, and radiated the parts of her body that smothered his whispers.

"Fine," she said.

There were seven people in line to get devil's pies when Philonia got back from the bank the morning after she attended Ava's women's group and the last time she saw Him. She walked behind the register and quickly put the money away, ready to take orders. Her "May I help you?" was interrupted when the woman she told to stay away dived over the counter, and again, grabbed Philonia by the collar. The rest happened quickly. Philonia felt two fiery smacks move across her face in rapid succession. She tried to wrestle the woman off of her, struggling to protect her face and to return blows. While the woman yelled, "stay out of our lives," she piled punches onto Philonia's back, driving her to the ground. Spread out woozy on the bakery tiles, Philonia thought of ashes and smoke. Then she saw two pairs of feet. Ava's white orthopedic soles and the woman's black leather boots skittered along the store tiles as people shouted for them to stop. Philonia clawed the counter to stand up and see her mother and her lover's wife fighting like amateur boxers whose lives depended on that win. As she started to run over to help Ava, two men intervened. They pulled the woman off of Ava and carried her out of the store, her legs flailing and knocking into chairs and appalled customers.

"Are you OK, Ms. Ava?" A few customers formed a circle around her. Others tried to tend to Philonia, who refused attention. She rushed to her mother and tried to soothe her, but didn't know which needed care first, the blood on her mother's lip or the swelling in her right hand.

"How does your wrist feel?" Philonia asked, while wishing they were the only ones in the store so she could tell her mother that she was sorry for getting her involved.

"Yes, I'll live," Ava said. "I told you she'd be back."

September sauntered in like it had been hiding cool air under her dress. Philonia decided to take a semester off and help her mother find a trustworthy, yet affordable bookkeeper. This gave her father ample time to plan elaborate evening walks. After the store would close, he'd take her through parts of the Bronx that she'd never seen before and he'd catch her up on his soaps.

"Did you think you were going to die?"

Skillman put both of his hands in the pockets of his khaki pants and jangled his keys. He led them toward a park bench, his eyes focused on his feet, and sat. His body hinged at the waist, knees, and elbows like a plastic doll.

"I know you know what I did," he said. "Your mother told me you've been in some trouble of your own."

"Do you still see Yvonne?" Her question flew out of her mouth and glided on the summer air, its cool rustle clean and absolute, like it would always stay that way even though it wouldn't.

"No."

"Do you still talk to her?"

"No," he said, crossing his legs at the ankles. "What more is there to say?"

Philonia thumbed the charm on her necklace and rose from the park bench. She looked down at him, wanting to answer, but beat back the urge, knowing that his question was rhetorical.

Philonia found a new wholesale sugar supplier that sold an organic brand that Ava really liked. She wanted to be a responsible shopper, so she checked to see if BJs sold it for less. They did.

Philonia loaded her cart with four bags of the new stuff and got in line to check out. She scanned the cashier's faces to see if she could spot Yvonne. A young man wearing an "associate in training" pin said that Yvonne got promoted to store manager. After Philonia paid, she asked where she could find her.

"How can I help you today?" Yvonne asked, chin raised, voice full of exuberance. Yvonne wore the same blinged out blue eyeshadow that caught Philonia's attention the day they met. She wore polyester slacks that fell straight to the soles of her work boots.

"Tell me you know her name."

A Closed Circuit

Tara Isabel Zambrano

[This flash piece reminds us of the many ways we've all been "washed in loneliness." A heartbreaking portrait of isolation and love, "A Closed Circuit" grapples with the question of what it means to desire and be desired. — AM]

My husband says I am out of love. He claims there is an empty space two fingers down my ribcage where love used to be. So he goes out with other women. When he returns: he cleans the house, puts on music, showers for long. His skin glows, his teeth shine. Sometimes my husband cries and talks in his sleep. I interlace my fingers with his and whisper, *I understand.* But he pulls away as if he can't stand the vacuum that oozes out of me. Lying next to him I smell a woman I used to know but can't recall her name. Was it Claire, Judy, Raina? Doesn't matter, it makes me wild, it turns me on: this dream, a culmination of all the women he has loved. It fills the void, makes me giggle. My husband wakes up, presses his hand under my bust, feels the flutter and confesses he does it all for us: to feel this moment together.

Sometimes the dream rises like smoke from my husband's cigarette, forms a funnel: a cone of faces revolving around him. Blondes, redheads and brunettes. Lost and beautiful. When my husband emerges, he looks brand new, a man ready to seduce again. He dyes his hair, wears contact lenses, and finds a different girl. Buys her expensive clothes and jewelry, slow dances with her until she cracks open like an egg, and spills her cravings in a cheap motel in the middle of nowhere. He brings her home. Together they watch movies, eat popcorn and fall asleep on the couch. I slip away, from the house into the streets and parks, washed in loneliness, sitting in my car, as the dusks flow into nights. My husband swears he never makes love to other women because he wants to stay loyal to me. *Commitment is what we live for*, he says. Eventually, the girl leaves him. Her scent, her longing to find true love, her wish to be remembered, all becomes a part of the dream.

The dream gets stronger, its grip tighter around our souls. A closed circuit.

My husband asserts he wants me to get better, to become a woman whose body is a large, beautiful bird: soft and accessible, whose heart explodes with love and understanding. The hope in his eyes makes me dizzy. I carve out cardboard wings, attach to my loose kaftan and flap in front of the mirror. I try to feel a movement in between my breath, a rush of color on my cheeks. Nothing. Usual rise and fall of my chest. *Thump thump* of my heart. The woman in the mirror raises an eyebrow at me. In the background, my husband winces.

Five weeks in a row, my husband gets red roses for the girl he is seeing. I soak in the warmth of their rich color that rises like a giant bubble and settles in the empty space inside me. I'm making progress, I exclaim but he doesn't believe me. *The dream is the cure*, he says, running his fingers over a rosebud, tight and tender like a rolled tongue.

My husband takes a break between dating girls. Those nights are the hardest. I ask him about signs of love and his silence sweeps through me. As days go by, I feel less sure about who I am. He promises things will recover: one day, he'll hold my hand for hours, paint my fingernails, massage my scalp, tongue-kiss between my legs, raise kids. The way he says this makes me believe it. Or want to.

Intermittently I worry if we'll run out of girls, if my husband will no longer have the passion to fill my bareness. If I'll never carry in my womb what I want to know about love, and pass it on. But he is always ready as if there is nothing else for him to do. As if finding another girl is as involuntary as his breathing. As if he needs the dream more than I do. As if I'm not the one out of love, I never was.

February Girl

Lisa Forrest

[We loved this piece for its understanding of how a single scene can be a window into an entire life. Its dreamy precision gives it the afterglow of memory—the writer's, and now ours too. — GRR]

He told her he liked the way the sunlight made her hair sparkle. They were sitting in his mother's pink and turquoise kitchen. There were pink roses on everything— the curtains, the chair cushions, the napkin holder—even the toaster and blender sat draped in rose printed covers. He said he wanted to take her photo because of the way the sunlight was hitting her hair—it was just perfect, and he liked how it covered one of her eyes. The man left the room to get his camera and the girl smoothed her long blonde hair. Outside there was nothing but new snow piled on top of old snow—the weight of it all brought a heavy quietness to the afternoon. The furnace kicked in again, and the girl thought of how the man's mother would sit on the living room floor in front of the heating vent. Every morning the man's mother sat there, curled like a house cat, reading her bible. Sometimes, the distant sound of a woman sobbing low-crawled slowly up the heat duct into the upstairs bedroom where the girl slept, filling the room with the saddest chill. It had been almost two months since the man's father had collapsed over the back of his desk chair, his hand to his heart. He was fresh from his bath, wearing his plaid flannel bathrobe, his best suit waiting on the bed. The girl remembered that night, after they had returned from the hospital with nothing more to say, the man's mother had vacuumed the carpets before the pastor arrived. The man was standing before her now, head down and fumbling with his camera lens—"*Can you put your hair back over one eye?*"

I Cannot Explain My Heart

Ayse Papatya Bucak

[Love and people are complicated, and "I Cannot Explain My Heart" knows this in every line. In this piece, Ayse Bucak gives fresh imagery and meaning to one of literature's most widespread symbols of devotion. What we would all give to be loved by a Godzilla heart! —PL]

Some days, my heart is in my head. It does not have a mind of its own. It thinks too much, I think.

Who doesn't want a wild and crazy heart, an untamed heart, a heart that cannot heal and at the same time cannot hurt? Some days, my heart is a cold heart, a hard heart, a hard-hatted heart.

But some days!

I am telling you, it is not.

I will take my heart into my own hands, I think. Somebody has to. Some people have told it no, and so I have told it no, but my heart, disobedient dog, will not lie down. It's no tight fist pumping in my rib cage. It's a six-fingered daisy (loves me, loves me not) on the long arm of a pendulum (love him, love him not) tucked in the dark end of a grandfather clock. It's a heart that won't stay still.

Once my nephew asked my mother what was my favorite thing in all of the world, and she said, books. If my nephew had asked me what my favorite thing in all of the world was, I would not have been able to answer.

Don't I know my own heart?

She was right. It is books.

Some days, I think the only reason I need other people is for them to write more books. But that is not true, of course.

I know women who say they knew they were dating the one! when he helped them through the death of, illness of, disaster of… But isn't it better to shore up against boredom than tragedy? Is love only the bookend to grief? Is love only in case of emergency? I just want a guy I want to talk to every day. That's a lie. I also want that guy to want to talk to me every day. No. Most days. I want us to want to talk to each other most days.

I may not be in love, but some days, I am in so much love I can't even tell you. I am inside of so much love.

At the Franklin Institute in Philadelphia, there is a large plastic heart for visitors to walk through. It used to be my favorite thing. Now, I see, it has seen better days. There is graffiti on the inside.

That is my heart. It has seen better days. But it's still a heart.

Walk through: you'll see. A working model of a heart!

My nephew was trying to figure out what to make me for my birthday. He wanted to make me my favorite thing in all of the world. So he made me a book. I did not think I could love him more than I did, but now I do. And then my niece was born. My god, my heart.

Some days, my heart feels like the tiny frog heart I excavated in seventh grade biology. But some days! It is a Godzilla heart.

You don't believe me, but I am telling you mine is a good heart. A heart-healthy heart. A candy red heart. A heart-shaped heart.

I will hand it over, I think. I've had it too long. You can have it.

That's a lie.

You already do. It's already gone. Look down. There it is, in your heart-shaped hands.

Contributors

Zea Archer is a writer and librarian living in New Jersey. Her poems, plays, and reviews have been read and performed in queer spaces, including *Skin to Skin*, *Your Name Here*, and *The Lesbrary*. Her nonfiction work on queer motherhood appears in *Hot Metal Bridge*, *Santa Fe Writers Project Quarterly*, and *Musepaper*, and was published in an anthology released by Read650. Her flash fiction appears in *The Bangalore Review*. You can follow her at www.archerzea.com

Darise Jean Baptiste is inspired by the Black women who raised her in the Bronx and St. Lucia. Currently living in Brooklyn and working in the social impact sector, she earned her MFA from Rutgers-Newark and her MA in English literature from Brooklyn College. Darise is a VONA and Callaloo Creative Writing Workshop alum. Her work is forthcoming at *Green Mountains Review*. You can follow her on Twitter @darisejean or at darisejeanbaptiste.com.

Ayşe Papatya Bucak is the author of *The Trojan War Museum and Other Stories* which was awarded the 2019 Spotlight Award by the Story Prize. Her writing has been published in a variety of journals including *One Story*, *Bomb*, *The Iowa Review*, *Guernica*, and *Witness*. Two of the stories from *The Trojan War Museum* were reprinted in the O. Henry and Pushcart Prize anthologies, and the collection was short-listed for the 2020 PEN/

Robert W. Bingham Award for a Debut Short Story Collection. She is an associate professor at Florida Atlantic University. You can follow her on Twitter @thefreemfa or www.aysebucak.com

Caroline Cabrera is the author of the lyric essay collection *(lack begins as a tiny rumble)* from Tinderbox Editions, as well as three poetry collections and two chapbooks, including most recently *The Coma of the Comet* from Burnside Review and *Saint X* from Black Lawrence Press. She is the Education Coordinator & Managing Editor at O, Miami. She is founder and editor of Bloom Books and cohost of the arts advice podcast *Now that We're Friends*. You can find her online at carolinecabrera.work

Alejandro Escudé's first book of poems, "My Earthbound Eye," was published in September 2013 upon winning the 2012 Sacramento Poetry Center Award. He received a master's degree in creative writing from UC Davis, where he was taught by such notable poets as Gary Snyder and Sandra McPherson. Alejandro works as an English teacher, having taught in a variety of school systems at the secondary level for over fifteen years. Originally from Córdoba, Argentina, he immigrated to California many years ago at the age of six. A new book, "The Book of the Unclaimed Dead," published by Main Street Rag Press, is now available on the MSR website. Alejandro is a single dad of two wonderful kids and lives in Los Angeles with his dog, a feisty yet lovable Jack Russell named Jake. You can find him online at www.escudepoetry.com

Lisa A. Forrest serves as the Leland M. Park Director of the Davidson College Library in Davidson, North Carolina. Her creative writing has been featured in publications such as the *Buffalo News*, *Damn the Caesars*, *eco-poetics*, *elimae*, *Hineni Magazine*, *Kadar Koli*, *The Volta*, *WordWrights*, and *Yellow Edenwald Field*. Lisa's collection of poems, *To the Eaves*, is available from BlazeVox Books. You can find her online @LisaAForrest.

Ángel García, a proud son of Mexican immigrants, is the author of *Teeth Never Sleep* (University of Arkansas Press), winner of a 2018 CantoMundo Poetry Prize, winner of a 2019 American Book Award from the Before Columbus Foundation, and finalist for the 2019 PEN America Open Book Award and 2020 Kate Tufts Discovery Award. His work can be found in *American Poetry Review*, *Crab Orchard Review*, *Waxwing*, *Huizache*, *Miramar*, and *The Good Men Project*, among others. He currently teaches at the University of Illinois at Urbana-Champaign. You can find him online @buffalopoet11 or www.angelgarciapoet.com.

Jennifer Harvey is a Scottish writer now living in Amsterdam. She is the author of three novels: 'Someone Else's Daughter' (Bookouture, June 2020), 'All The Lies We Told' (Bookouture, October 2020), and a third title, forthcoming in May 2021. Her short fiction has appeared in various publications in the US and the UK, including: *Carve*, *Folio*, *Bare Fiction*, *The Lonely Crowd*, *New Writing Scotland 38*, and *Best Short Fiction 2020*. She is a Resident Reader for *Carve Magazine*, and serves as a member of the Editorial Board for *Ellipsis Magazine*. When not writing, she can be found sauntering along the Amsterdam canals, dreaming up new stories. You can find her online over at www.jenharvey.net or follow her on Twitter @JenAnneHarvey1.

Adalena Kavanagh is a writer, photographer and librarian in Brooklyn. She has published interviews and stories in *Believer Magazine* and *The Literary Review*. She just completed a novel. You can follow her on Twitter @adalenakavanagh.

Sally Rosen Kindred is the author of *No Eden* and *Book of Asters* from

Mayapple Press, and *Where the Wolf*, winner of the 2020 Diode Book Prize and forthcoming from Diode Editions in 2021. Her poems have appeared in *The Gettysburg Review*, *Shenandoah*, *The Missouri Review*'s Poem-of-the-week web feature, and *Kenyon Review* Online. She lives in Maryland. You can find her online @SallyRKindred or sallyrosenkindred.com.

Gregory Lawless is the author of *Far Away* (Red Mountain Press, 2015) and *Dreambugh, Pennsylvania* (forthcoming from Dream Horse Press).

Sally Wen Mao is the author of *Oculus* (Graywolf Press, 2019), a finalist for the Los Angeles Times Book Prize for poetry, and Mad Honey Symposium (Alice James Books, 2014). Mao was a 2016-2017 fellow at the Cullman Center for Scholars and Writers at the New York Public Library, the 2017-2018 Jenny McKean Moore Writer-in-Washington at George Washington University, and a 2021 Black Mountain Institute Shearing fellow. You can find her online @sallywenmao or sallywenmao.com.

Oliver de la Paz is the author of five collections of poetry, *Names Above Houses*, *Furious Lullaby* (SIU Press 2001, 2007), *Requiem for the Orchard* (U. of Akron Press 2010, winner of the Akron Prize for poetry chosen by Martìn Espada), *Post Subject: A Fable* (U. of Akron Press 2014), and the forthcoming book *The Boy in the Labyrinth* (U. of Akron Press 2019). He is the co-editor with Stacey Lynn Brown of *A Face to Meet the Faces: An Anthology of Contemporary Persona Poetry* (U. of Akron Press 2012). He co-chairs the advisory board of Kundiman, a not-for-profit organization dedicated to the promotion of Asian American Poetry and is a former member of the Board of Trustees for the Association of Writers and Writing Programs. A recipient of a NYFA Fellowship Award and a GAP Grant from Artist Trust, his work has appeared in journals like *Virginia Quarterly Review*, *North American Review*, *Tin House*, *Poetry*, and in anthologies such as *Asian American Poetry: The Next Generation*. He teaches at the College of the Holy Cross and in the Low-Residency MFA Program at Pacific Lutheran University. You can find him online @Oliver_delaPaz or www.oliverdelapaz.com

Craig Santos Perez is the author of five books of poetry and the co-editor of five anthologies. He is a professor in the English department at the University of Hawaii, Manoa. You can find him online at craigsantosperez.com.

Marissa Schwalm lives in Andover, MA and teaches English at Phillips Academy - Andover. She has spent the previous eleven years teaching at the college level, and working as an editor and faculty advisor for various literary magazines. You can find her online @MarissaSchwalm.

Hannah Soyer is a queer disabled writer interested in exploring representations of othered bodies. Her work has appeared in *Cosmopolitan*, *Entropy*, *Mikrokosmos Journal*, *Brain Mill Press*, *Disability Visibility Project*, and *Rooted in Rights*, among other places. She is the founder of This Body is Worthy, a project aimed at celebrating bodies outside of mainstream societal ideals, and Words of Reclamation, a space for disabled writers. Hannah also happens to be a cat and chocolate enthusiast.

Pablo Piñero Stillmann has been the recipient of Mexico's two top grants for young writers: The Foundation for Mexican Literature (FLM) and The National Fund for Culture and Arts (FONCA). His fiction, nonfiction and poetry have appeared in, among other journals, *Bennington Review*, *Sycamore Review*, *Notre Dame Review* and *Washington Square Review*. He is the author of a novel, *Temblador* (Tierra Adentro,

2014), and a short story collection, *Our Brains and the Brains of Miniature Sharks* (Moon City Press, 2020). You can find him online @p_p_st or www.pablopst.com.

Qinglan Wang is a multilingual writer and artist originally from Hawaii. Nominated for a Pushcart Prize (2012), her work has been featured in *Fourth Genre, Ninth Letter, The Ocean State Review*, among other places. She received her MFA from George Mason University. More information available at www.qinglanwang.net

David E. Yee is an Asian American writer whose work has appeared in *American Short Fiction, AGNI Online, Seneca Review, Gulf Coast Online*, and elsewhere. In 2017, he won the *New Ohio Review* Fiction Contest, judged by Colm Tóibín, as well as the Press 53 Flash Contest judged by Jeffrey Condran. He's a bartender in Columbus, Ohio.

Tara Isabel Zambrano is the author of *Death, Desire And Other Destinations*, a full-length flash collection by OKAY Donkey Press. Her work has won the first prize in *The Southampton Review* Short Short Fiction Contest 2019, a second prize in Bath Flash Award 2020, been a Finalist in Bat City Review 2018 Short Prose Contest and *Mid-American Review* Fineline 2018 Contest. Her flash fiction has been published in *The Best Small Fictions 2019, The Best Micro Fiction 2019, 2020* Anthology. She lives in Texas and is the Fiction Editor for *Waxwing Literary Journal*. You can find her online @theinnerzone.

Acknowledgments

All pieces were previously published on hotmetalbridge.org

From the author of "Fractured Composition" (pg 97) Jennifer Harvey: "This story will be reprinted in the 2020 Best Small Fictions Anthology published by Sonder Press also under the title "Fractured Composition."

Thank you to Chuck Kinder.

www.ingramcontent.com/pod-product-compliance
Lightning Source LLC
Chambersburg PA
CBHW030827200726
48285CB00007B/2383